ICU

Jamel A. Moore, Sr.

Copyright © 2025 by Jamel A. Moore, Sr.

Published by

Kingdom Connected

Toms River, NJ

ISBN 979-8-218-82021-3

All rights reserved. No part of this book may be reproduced in any form or by any electronic or mechanical means, including information storage and retrieval systems, without written permission from the author, except for the use of brief quotations in a book review.

Dedication

This book is dedicated to every individual who's ever felt irrelevant, isolated, or invisible. God cares. God knows. God sees.

Contents

Acknowledgments	vii
Foreword	ix
1. Don't Wash Your Hands of It Just Yet	1
2. Rescued from a Routine	8
3. Paralyzed by Procrastination	15
4. Don't Dry Out	22
5. The Imprint of Certainty	27
6. The Celebration of Being Found	32
7. Rejoicing In Rejection	36
8. 'Tis The Season For A Pep Talk	43
9. I've Been Rocked, But I'm Still Rolling	51
10. Withdrawals and Deposits	55
11. A Rest Stop For The Restless	63
12. Closed Doors Don't Matter	71

Acknowledgments

I want to thank my pastor for upwards of 30 years, Archbishop Eric R. Figueroa, Sr., for always seeing the best in me when others saw the worst in me, and even those moments when I couldn't see the forest for the trees. You continued to say it, and now I finally see it!

Foreword

Dr. Jamel A. Moore, Sr. is a miraculous specimen of divine intervention! After suffering renal failure, he is a two-time recipient, of Kidney transplants! His experiences on dialysis over the years has given him a powerful perspective, and keen insight on how illness can affect your psyche.

I.C.U. is an inspirational triage, examining some of the physical cases that address healing, in the scriptures. It offers a tangible reveal of God's ability to restore the health, and the wholeness, of those who have been physically afflicted.

The inevitability of sickness, and disease, and pain, and possibly even the threat of death, makes ICU a relevant read! The reality is that all of us, will probably pay a visit to ICU, before our days are done.

Read ICU, and familiarize yourself with a Dr, who is not just a general practitioner, but a specialist who specializes in every ailment common to the human condition! ICU will encourage you to manage your infirmity, in expectation, and anticipation, of divine healing!

Congratulations on your selection of ICU. I wholeheartedly

Foreword

recommend this book as a worthwhile read! ".. and with His stripes we are healed!" (Isaiah 53:5)

Be Blessed, Be Healed, And Be Delivered!

Dr. Eric R. Figueroa, Sr.

Don't Wash Your Hands of It Just Yet

Luke 5:1-2
And it came to pass that, as the people pressed upon him to hear the word of God, he stood by the lake of Gennesaret, and saw two ships standing by the lake: but the fishermen were gone out of them, and were washing their nets.

Ever since the detection of the COVID-19 virus in 2020, there has been an intense emphasis on the importance of washing our hands. Everywhere you looked, there were signs instructing us on how to effectively and efficiently sanitize. As things have vastly improved concerning the pandemic, there has been a reduced awareness of the demand to keep our hands clean.

The old adage says, "Cleanliness is next to godliness." No, this isn't Scripture, but it is a principle on how essential it is to keep your hands clean. David asks and answers in Psalm 24: *"Who shall ascend into the hill of the Lord? Or who shall stand in his holy place? He that hath clean hands, and a pure heart…"* What an intriguing prerequisite, that anyone selected to experience an encounter of worship with God must live a righteous life. You recall the verse from the baptism anthem "Take Me to the Water": *"None but the righteous shall see God."*

Truth be told, I don't need another news report, a warning about spreading diseases, or a sign in a restroom to remind me of the benefits of washing my hands before I cook, go in the refrigerator, come from outside, or especially after using the bathroom. That was taught to me at home. The method of vigorously washing your hands diminishes germs and infections. Glory to God!

But let me pause and inform you that this is not about washing your hands in the natural sense. Follow my thought process as I discuss our approach to washing our hands in the spiritual sense.

No matter what time of the year you're reading this, I know you've been praying, fasting, singing, and sowing, believing God for what He has promised. The trials you've faced have not just tested your faith but also revealed a lot about who you are. This is exactly what tests are designed to do: gauge what you know, reveal what you don't know, and disclose who you really are. Sometimes you don't know what you can handle until you've personally gone through it yourself.

I can't speak for anybody else, but in the words of Kirk Franklin and God's Property: "I've gone through the fire. I've been through the flood. I've been broken into pieces. Seen lightning flashing from above." I'm so glad Jesus will never put more on me than I can bear. So, when a package of circumstances arrives at your doorstep, sign for it and know it's been sent by God, who understands your capacity to survive.

You remember our brother John in Revelation, banished to the island of Patmos for the word of God and his testimony of Jesus Christ. He survived being put in a pot of boiling oil because the oil wouldn't boil. Daniel survived overnight in a lion's den where ferocious beasts were positioned to destroy him because of his faithfulness to God. Isaiah 43:2 *confirms, "When thou passest through the waters, I will be with thee; and through the rivers, they shall not overflow thee: when thou walkest through the fire, thou shalt not be burned; neither shall the flame kindle upon thee."* Just as Daniel and John both survived, I'm looking for you to survive!

I'm almost positive you've heard the phrase, "Don't throw the baby out with the bathwater." This figure of speech means that while getting rid of something unwanted, one could also eliminate something good or valuable. In one way or another, we are all guilty of this. Depending on our mood or mindset, we can discard precious pieces in our haste to be done with a situation once and for all.

This is a good place to remind you, beloved, that everything has worth because when God made it, He saw and said, *"It was good."* Everyone also has value because the psalmist reminds us, *"We are fearfully and wonderfully made."* James 1:17 shares, *"Every good gift and every perfect gift is from above."* So, what's garbage to you can be treasure to someone else.

On the other side of the coin, the theme song of the 1978 classic sitcom *Diff'rent Strokes* says, "What might be right for you may not be right for some." Hebrews 13:2 notes, *"Be not forgetful to entertain strangers: for thereby some have entertained angels unawares."* We've all been created differently, but by the same God. If God made us all alike, it would limit His versatility, and we know that's not the case. Some of our characteristics can offend and turn people away, while others can attract them, because opposites do indeed attract. You'll never know what people bring to the table if they're never invited to the table. God strategically allows us to cross paths with people for events, episodes, and eternity. Once we discover what category they belong to, it will save us from a lifetime of headaches and heartaches.

We as humans often connect with individuals who have reached the status of being everyone's favorite before we consider those who are truly the favored of God. Sometimes it's how they're packaged and presented that distracts us from who really carries the goods. For example, Jacob found himself in a love triangle between two sisters, Rachel and Leah. Rachel's popularity was based on breathtaking beauty. She was a combination of Beyoncé, Jennifer Lopez, and Thanksgiving dinner.

Meanwhile, her older sister Leah was described in the Bible as "tender-eyed." In other words, she was cross-eyed, one eye looking where she was going, and one eye going where she was looking. Jacob wasn't interested in Leah because they couldn't see eye to eye.

But it wasn't just looks that separated the sisters. Rachel was barren, while Leah could produce. The moral of the story: despite how I look on the outside, it's what's going on inside that really counts. Take a moment and declare to yourself, "I might not be popular, but Lord, I just want to be productive!" Life has taught us that favored outshines favorite every time. David pens in Psalm 41:11: *"By this I know that thou favourest me, because mine enemy doth not triumph over me."*

On another occasion, it was Mark, not Silas, that Paul originally desired to take with him on the missionary journey because of Mark's résumé. Mark is described in *2 Timothy* as being "profitable for ministry." But despite those glowing accolades, Mark didn't have the paperwork to travel to Rome. So, Paul took Silas, who was more equipped for the challenges of ministry. This proved to be the perfect decision, because in *Acts 16*, at midnight, it was Paul and Silas who prayed and sang praises in a Roman prison. They were loosed because of good behavior.

In one of my sermons, I preached about the wheat and the tares. The servant recognized tares among the wheat and wanted to pull them up, but his master warned him that pulling the tares could damage the wheat. And how can we forget Pontius Pilate, who washed his hands of the debate concerning the release of Barabbas or Jesus. Pilate knew the status of the two men: Barabbas, a convicted criminal, and Jesus, an innocent man. Yet he left the fatal decision in the hands of a biased crowd instead of using his authority to do what was right. Doesn't that sound familiar?

We, too, are guilty of dismissing people too quickly, refusing to give them time to develop, grow, and mature. We absolve ourselves from the burden of accountability and responsibility. But we soon learn, just like Jacob, Paul, the servant in the field, and Pilate, what my mother instilled in me as a child: "It's better to have and not need, than to need and not have." Or as the saying goes, "You never miss your water until the well runs dry."

So, before you cut off, ignore, or stop speaking to those you feel are insignificant or unnecessary, I urge you to H.A.L.T. Never make a decision when you're Hungry, Angry, Lonely, or Tired. You never know who or what God has placed in your life as the answer to your prayer, the tool for your next victory, or the catalyst for your next miracle.

You remember the rich man who mishandled and mistreated Lazarus while they were alive. Ironically, when they both died, Lazarus went to Heaven, and the rich man went to Hell. The rich man begged Abraham to allow Lazarus to dip his finger in water to cool his tongue from the anguish of the flames.

And let me remind you, time will square some things away. You've heard the saying, "Time heals all wounds." As seconds turn into minutes, minutes into hours, hours into days, days into weeks, weeks into months, and months into years, grief eventually dissipates. Time will cause you to rethink issues. Time will help you see others in a different light. Time will birth apologies and forgiveness. And time will prove that you never know who you'll need when you're in a bind.

So don't take time for granted. Please don't let pride cause you to forfeit who and what you need in this season.

Imagine if the heroes of the Bible had dismissed the weapons God gave them as inadequate. What if Moses destroyed his rod after Pharaoh's magicians turned theirs into snakes? Yet it was that rod that parted the Red Sea. What if David dismissed his slingshot as a child's toy instead of using it to defeat Goliath? What if Samson underestimated the jawbone of a donkey? What if Esther allowed her gender and the threat of death to silence her? And what if Jesus never conceded His will to die for us in the Garden of Gethsemane? We wouldn't have the promise of eternal life.

Our choices are critical. They affect not only us but also our bloodline and storyline. Attached to every choice are consequences and rewards.

Let me close with the text recorded in *Luke 5*. Jesus was teaching at the lake of Gennesaret, where He found two ships unoccupied because the fishermen had gone out to wash their nets. This might have seemed routine to some, but to Jesus it was significant. The men parked their boats and washed their nets after an unsuccessful voyage, frustrated because they came back empty-handed. These were master fishermen who had all the skill, tools, and preparation to succeed, yet they still failed. Washing their nets symbolized giving up.

How often do we start the year with resolutions? Saving money, losing weight, breaking habits, only to find ourselves unfulfilled by October, parked on the shore with our nets washed?

But I'm here to tell you, don't wash your hands of it just yet. Jesus is on the scene, and my Bible says, *"With men it is impossible, but with God all things are possible."* Have you any mountains that seem impossible to tunnel through? Any rivers that seem uncrossable? God specializes in things that seem impossible, and He will do what no other power can do.

Yes, the boats still have value, and the nets still have worth. If you keep reading, Jesus gave the fishermen inspiration to try again. And when they did, they were blessed with more than they could handle. The boats carried the blessing, and the nets caught the blessing.

ICU

So, I'm here to tell you, continue to believe, and try again. I know you were ready to wash your hands of it because of emotions, embarrassment, and emptiness. But the Holy Spirit sent me to stop you in your haste and tap you on the shoulder with two words: *Not yet.*

Rescued from a Routine

St. Mark 10:46-52

And they came to Jericho: and as he went out of Jericho with his disciples and a great company of people, blind Bartimaeus, the son of Timaeus, sat by the highway side begging. And when he heard that it was Jesus of Nazareth, he began to cry out, and say, Jesus, thou son of David, have mercy on me. And many charged him that he should hold his peace: but he cried the more a great deal, Thou son of David, have mercy on me. And Jesus stood still, and commanded him to be called. And they called the blind man, saying unto him, Be of good comfort, rise; he calleth thee. And he, casting away his garment, rose, and came to Jesus. And Jesus answered and said unto him, What wilt thou that I should do unto thee? The blind man said unto him, Lord, that I might receive my sight. And Jesus said unto him, Go thy way; thy faith hath made thee whole. And immediately he received his sight, and followed Jesus in the way.

In 1966, a newcomer to the music business, Fontella Bass, introduced the world to the hit classic "Rescue Me." For years, even up to this present day, some have been thoroughly

ICU

convinced that Aretha Franklin is the iconic voice behind the song. Make no mistake: that signature sound we all remember is the legendary Fontella Bass. Who can forget the infamous commercial with the old lady on the floor yelling, "I've fallen, and I can't get up!" She needed somebody to rescue her.

As we consider the word rescue, it literally means to save someone from a dangerous or distressing situation. Whether we like to admit it or not, all of us at one point or another have had to be rescued, whether from toxic relationships, a financial rut, a life-or-death situation, or simply the need for sound advice on how to escape a disaster or dilemma.

Down through the years, we've seen countless fictional heroes step in to save the day. Lois Lane is helped by Superman after falling from the top of a 70-story building. Spider-Man swoops in to stop a runaway train full of frantic passengers. Batman and Robin save a damsel in distress from the evil plans of the Joker, Penguin, or the Riddler. Mighty Mouse shows up just in the nick of time. These heroes are proficient at saving the day, but being rescued can leave you dependent, helpless, and vulnerable. Those who are used to being independent have a difficult time adjusting to dependency. In times of crisis, ego and pride must take a backseat, and survival must be prioritized. Am I talking right?

Often, independent people don't like to ask for help. It goes against their moral compass. They would rather go without than ask for assistance and risk being reminded later that they needed help. There's nothing worse than showing transparency, getting relief, and then hearing from a so-called savior, "You wouldn't be where you are without me." That's not real help. Those people are opportunists. They take your information and use it for ammunition. It's important to ask God to surround you with the right support to avoid that kind of betrayal. I learned that everyone you can count on, you can't always count on. That's why I must tell Jesus, because I can't bear these burdens alone. If you have a little talk with Jesus, tell him all about your trouble. He'll hear your faintest cry, and he'll answer by and by. You'll feel the prayer wheel turning and know the fire is burning. Just have a little talk with Jesus, and he'll make it right.

The text above is found in the Gospel according to St. Mark. Mark gives us a front-row seat to Jesus as a servant. Matthew reminds us, *"He that is greatest among you shall be your servant."* Paul echoes the same sentiment in Philippians 2:7, where Jesus Christ "took on the form of a servant." Though existing in the form of God, he voluntarily emptied himself and became a servant, born in the likeness of men. This is an act of humility and self-sacrifice: the divine choosing to become human to identify with and save humanity. I'm glad I have a high priest who can be touched with the feelings of my infirmity. Can you relate?

Jesus was a servant. Are you a servant? Do you know any servants? People who would rather serve than be served, who find more joy in giving than receiving? "If I can help somebody as I travel along, then my living won't be in vain." You've got to be mindful of whom you release power to and, more importantly, whom you give power in your life. Remember, I'm not Jane, and you're not Tarzan. Don't swing in and out of my life because you view me as handicapped and needing a handout. Herod, Nebuchadnezzar, and Pharaoh were kings who abused their power and were considered tyrants. Even though Jesus had power, he never allowed it to go to his head. I'm so glad I serve a Christ who's more concerned about my inventory than his authority. Hallelujah!

In chapter 10, we're introduced to a blind man named Bartimaeus in the region of Jericho. You know it was through Joshua's obedience that the walls of Jericho came tumbling down. The older I become, the more I realize what a blessing it is to be able to see. Pass it down your row: don't take your eyes for granted. You may be suffering from cataracts, glaucoma, blurry vision, be farsighted or nearsighted, or be required to wear glasses. Thank God for the ability to see. Usually, individuals who are blind are accustomed to darkness and shadows; they become dependent and are often led. A seeing-eye dog may be assigned, and a walking cane can help detect objects in the way. Despite not being able to see, a blind person can still read using Braille and accomplish great things. Helen Keller, Ray Charles, and Stevie Wonder are templates who should inspire you: being disabled doesn't mean you're disqualified.

We must be mindful in days of darkness of whom we follow. In the height of our "see nothing" moments, whose directions are you following? Matthew 15:14 warns, *"They be blind leaders of the blind. And if the blind lead the blind, both shall fall into the ditch."* I hear the hymn writer sing, "Twas blind, but now I see." Mark also notes that this blind man is the "son of Timaeus," which means "honor" or "highly prized." It's amazing that one's lineage can be categorized as honorable, yet the person remains in a low place. It just doesn't add up.

Have you ever been in a low place? Low self-esteem, low income, low self-worth? Often our circumstances are just a low-down, dirty shame. Psalm 138 comforts us: *"If I ascend up into heaven, thou art there: if I make my bed in hell, behold, thou art there."* Wherever you are at this very moment, the Lord is right there with you. Ain't that good news? Not only is his presence guaranteed, but his blood is not deterred by distance. It reaches the highest mountain and flows to the lowest valley. The blood that gives me strength from day to day will never lose its power. Thank God for the determination of the blood.

Mark goes further and mentions that Bartimaeus is not just blind and connected to royalty, but he's also a beggar on the highway. Being a beggar requires intentional communication. It's got to be more than a sign you hold up or a can you hold out. Your plight and presentation must be so convincing that others are persuaded to share their hard-earned money. Some beggars we meet may have suffered life-changing injuries that hinder employment; others may be bound to a wheelchair due to disability. While some stories are legitimate, others are professional con artists and scammers.

Let me tell you this quick story: my bishop and I were driving down Atlantic Avenue and stopped at a light. A beggar came and wanted to wipe the windows for spare change. The rag was filthy, so the bishop declined. The man then asked for a dollar. The bishop said he only had a $20 bill. The gentleman pulled out a wad of singles and said, "Don't worry, I got change." On another occasion, I was in KFC to get a quick snack and was approached by a man who claimed he hadn't eaten in three days. I wasn't going to give him money because I'm not contributing to a habit, but I offered to buy him something to eat. He told me he wasn't a fan of KFC; he preferred Popeyes. I reminded him he was in the wrong chicken place. That's why you have to be discerning about who you help and how you treat others in those situations: you could be entertaining angels unaware, or you can fall prey to schemes.

This man's location is key to our lesson. The highway side was a high-traffic area, a spot full of opportunities to fulfill his agenda. This was his everyday routine. You may have a routine too: coffee before starting the morning, the same route daily, the same meal every Wednesday, the same bedtime, the same five friends, the same set offering in church, the same order at a restaurant. While some habits seem harmless and even produce good results, we can also be faithful to dysfunction because old habits die hard.

This blind beggar had resolved that begging was his best option for stability. He's a tad different from the beggar in *Acts 3* because of his blindness and his place of request. In *Acts 3*, the beggar was at the gate called Beautiful. Is it possible to be in a beautiful place physically and be in an ugly place socially or spiritually at the same time? Both beggars had routines and sought financial assistance, but the one in Acts received a pick-me-up from Peter and John (the disciples) while the other one was in the presence of Jesus Christ, the ultimate picker-upper. There may be failure in a disciple, but there's no failure in our God.

If you continue to do things the same way, you're bound to get the same results. I've discovered that when one of your senses isn't working at full capacity, the other senses are heightened. When I can't see my way, when bitterness sits on my tongue, when I experience the absence of a touch and the aroma of avoidance fills the air, somehow I can still hear. The Apostle Paul reminds us, *"Faith cometh by hearing; for we walk by faith, and not by sight."* I heard the joyful sound that Jesus saves. He will pick you up and turn you around. Hallelujah, Jesus saves!

Let me close this chapter and leave you with this: the man heard Jesus was in the vicinity. I wonder, with all the static in your life, can you still hear Jesus? When folks are offering opinions, when people give their two cents, and you still come up short, when those who should be egging you on try to silence you, and when you realize this may be your last chance for a change, you ought to forget them and cry out to him. Take a moment, close your eyes, and scream, "Lord, please don't pass me by!" Get God's attention. Cause Jesus to stand still.

Mark shows us that every action causes a reaction: if, after you call his name, he answers, then he'll call your name back. Aren't you glad God knows your name? *Simon, Simon. I prayed for you! Lazarus, come forth! Bartimaeus, receive your sight!* As you read this, he's calling your name. Yes! I know when he called you in times past, you were too busy doing you. In times past, you may not have recognized his voice. In times past, you sent him to voicemail. Today he's calling again, your name, but under dire circumstances. When he calls this time, take off those old garments. When he calls, be willing to say, "I want to see, see clearly, see it his way, see the light." *I saw the light; I saw the light. No more darkness, no more night. Now I'm so happy, no sorrow in sight.* Praise the Lord. When he calls, let Jesus know you're ready to be rescued from your routine -- the tired, the mundane, the same old, same old.

If you've been signaling for help, help is now here. In Bible days, there was a routine for atonement: sacrifices of calves, goats, and lambs by the priests. After a while, that blood was no longer sufficient. Something had to give. An alternative was required; we needed rescue from the burden of sin once and for all. What was the solution? Is there a plan? The world was dying for a remedy. *For God so loved the world, that he gave his only begotten Son, that whosoever believeth in him should not perish, but have everlasting life.* His birth was our passageway, his life our pattern, his death our pardon, and his blood our petition. You don't have to kill the lamb anymore. And what can wash away my sins? Nothing but the blood of Jesus. What can make me whole again? Nothing but the blood of Jesus. Oh, precious is that flow that makes me white as snow. No other fount I know. Nothing but the blood of Jesus. Someone has taken the place of the lamb. He has rescued us from the routine. A damaging routine, a deadly routine, a dismissing routine.

I challenge you to do what Peter did when he was sinking fast: shout, "Lord, help me!" Scream, "Lord, save me!" Yell, "Lord, rescue me."

Paralyzed by Procrastination

St. John 5:1-9
After this there was a feast of the Jews, and Jesus went up to Jerusalem. Now there is at Jerusalem by the sheep market a pool, which is called in the Hebrew tongue Bethesda, having five porches. In these lay a great multitude of impotent folk, of blind, halt, withered, waiting for the moving of the water. For an angel went down at a certain season into the pool, and troubled the water: whosoever then first after the troubling of the water stepped in was made whole of whatsoever disease he had. And a certain man was there, which had an infirmity thirty and eight years. When Jesus saw him lie, and knew that he had been now a long time in that case, he saith unto him, Wilt thou be made whole? The impotent man answered him, Sir, I have no man, when the water is troubled, to put me into the pool: but while I am coming, another steppeth down before me. Jesus saith unto him, Rise, take up thy bed, and walk. And immediately the man was made whole, and took up his bed, and walked: and on the same day was the sabbath.

Jamel A. Moore, Sr.

In 1995, actor Christopher Reeve was thrown from a horse during an equestrian competition in Culpeper, Virginia, paralyzing him from the neck down. The accident occurred when he landed on his helmet at a near-perpendicular angle, breaking two neck vertebrae and damaging nerve fibers. Although his spinal cord was not completely severed, he suffered a large hemorrhage at the injury site. The once agile superstar who played Superman, able to leap tall buildings in a single bound, more powerful than a locomotive, the Man of Steel, was now confined to a wheelchair. It is amazing how one tragedy can change a person's life forever.

Perhaps this tragic event has triggered some occasion in your life that may not have left you physically paralyzed, but emotionally and mentally paralyzed. I believe all of us are aware of the significant challenges a person who is disabled can experience. The dependence on others to aid them daily, the inability to move around freely, the numerous doctors' appointments, and medications that now fill their schedule can be aggravating and frustrating. It is one thing to be pushed around, but it is another thing to be a pushover.

Can you begin to imagine the emotional strain and mental pain on an individual who is paralyzed without the presence of a wheelchair? Life, dear friends, can leave you in an immobile place. It can rob you of your joy, steal your happiness, eliminate your passion, and take a toll on your heart. I know someone here today understands firsthand what I mean. When your heart is numb, it can be extremely difficult to give love and to receive love. The emotional wall is a real thing, beloved. Many of us add a new brick every day. This force field is created to be a deterrent, built to protect the soul, but also to hinder those who try to get close.

Being paralyzed in any form can transform a person into a version of themselves they never imagined. That is the tone introduced in our text. In St. John chapter 5, the beloved disciple writes to us about a group of people who were paralyzed. The details of how they became statistics are not given, and truthfully, details can often be disturbing, but more importantly, they are usually a distraction. In this nosy society in which we live, people are more interested in the details than the deliverance. We often make the mistake of explaining the nooks and crannies of our dilemmas so thoroughly that we never get to a solution. We are left stuck, stagnant, stale, staring, and searching for answers.

These folk were stranded by the pool of Bethesda in Jerusalem. Jerusalem is often referred to as "The City of Peace." But isn't it ironic how you can be in a peaceful place, yet have no peace? One would think that because these people were by a pool, it must have been nice. Sadly, they were by it but had no strength to get into it. Why? John describes them as halt, withered, blind, and impotent. These diagnoses categorized them as patients in critical condition.

All these individuals in the great multitude were not just by the pool but sitting on the porch. Porches are places where people become stationary. If you grew up in a rural area, most houses had a porch. You might recall people sitting in a rocking chair, drinking lemonade or iced tea, enjoying the view. But this was not a comfortable surrounding. It was a contagious and contaminated environment. There was no access to a vaccine, their immunizations were not up to date, and disease filled the air. Every person who occupied a spot on the porch had potential.

There is nothing more heartbreaking than having potential stuck on the porch. We all know someone with tremendous potential, yet they are on the porch of "do nothing." They possess great ability but waste time talking instead of doing. They have future aspirations but are paralyzed by their past. It is not about what they are doing now, but what they are capable of becoming. We all should desire to become what God has in mind for us to be.

Jamel A. Moore, Sr.

I remember Bishop Figueroa once shared the acronym H.A.L.T. at New Life Tabernacle. He emphasized never make a decision when you are Hungry, Angry, Lonely, or Tired. We have all been guilty of this. Irrational decisions can leave us full of regrets. Esau forfeited his birthright to his brother Jacob because he was hungry after a hard day's work in the field. Moses struck the rock out of anger instead of speaking to the rock as God commanded when the children of Israel were complaining of thirst in the wilderness. Leah found herself in a cycle of dysfunction, lonely and looking for the love of a man. Samson shared the secret behind his amazing strength during pillow talk with Delilah. Brothers and sisters, have you ever made hasty moves because you did not take a moment to H.A.L.T.?

Blindness is another paralysis. You can see the errors of others but have cataracts and glaucoma concerning your own issues. We see what we want to see and choose to ignore what we do not want to face. The truth can be staring us right in the face, but because our reality is not a picture worth purchasing, we turn our attention to the flaws of others instead of putting our eyes on what really needs our attention. The Bible tells us that when the blind lead the blind, both fall into a ditch. Ray Charles and Stevie Wonder can see that change is needed. If you are honest with yourself, you see it too, but you do not see a strategy to get out of what you are in. Others can offer advice, suggestions, and give their two cents, but until you are willing to face it, God will not fix it. Tell yourself, "I've got to face it so God can fix it."

The phrase "impotent folk" refers to people who are weak, feeble, or lacking in power or strength. If we are honest with ourselves, two things can be true at the same time: you can be strong in some areas and weak in others. Every strong person has weak days. The devil assigns people to your life who will take advantage of your vulnerable condition. You become their target and their prey. They relish the chance to get the most out of you when you do not have the strength to fight back. But I want to speak into your life: get your fight back. You are more than a conqueror. God has invested the ingredients for your survival.

The last group of individuals at this pool were the withered, men and women who could not seem to get a grip on life. Have you ever felt like you lost your grip? You could not hold onto a job. Could not hold onto an apartment. Could not hold onto money. Things slip out of your hands faster than they come in.

As these people faced different scenarios, they were all in the same condition: paralyzed by procrastination. All of us have struggled, will struggle, or know someone who struggles with this plague. Fear of failure, scheduling conflicts, finances, or lack of support are just a few reasons people delay their destiny. Procrastination is putting off today what you think you can achieve tomorrow. While weighing the pros and cons, minutes become hours, hours become days, days become weeks, weeks become months, and before you know it, another year of unrealized resolutions has passed.

Paralysis can leave you with the three W's: Wondering, Wandering, and Worrying. You wonder, "How could a person like me wind up in a place like this?" Job put it plainly: *"For the thing which I greatly feared is come upon me, and that which I was afraid of is come unto me. I was not in safety, neither had I rest, neither was I quiet; yet trouble came"* (Job 3:25-26). Later, he wrote, *"Man that is born of a woman is of few days, and full of trouble"* (Job 14:1). But I am so glad trouble does not last always. Mahalia Jackson reminded us, "Soon I will be done with the troubles of the world and go home to be with the Lord."

Trouble can leave you wandering, going in circles, desperate and dizzy. The wilderness was never designed to be a holding cell; it was a passageway to the promised land. But 40 days turned into 40 years as murmuring and complacency grew louder. Wandering will take you down dark paths and bury you in pits you cannot climb out of. And wandering always leads to worrying. You look in the mirror and do not see a winner. You see someone disabled, handicapped, or crippled. But hear me: you may be disabled, but you are not disqualified.

These patients were waiting for the moving of water. Their healing was in the movement, but they were paralyzed by procrastination. God positions us for breakthroughs, yet we battle with movement. We fail to send the resume, fill out the application, show up for the interview, or answer the phone. But I want to encourage you today: it is your move. Not backward, but forward. The season of your paralysis is ending. You may think you are waiting on God, but beloved, God is waiting on you.

This man in the text had been in his condition for 38 years. That's over three decades of paralysis. And still, when Jesus asked him if he wanted to be made whole, he made excuses. *"Sir, I have no man, when the water is troubled, to put me into the pool."* Excuses. Excuses. Excuses. My junior high gym teacher used to say, "Excuses explain, but they don't excuse you." You may have legitimate reasons, but that does not erase the consequences.

In 2004, Christopher Reeve died from cardiac arrest, never able to walk again, and bound to a wheelchair. But as you read this, you should be saying to yourself, "That won't be me. I've had tragic events, but my story won't end like this." There is a happy ending waiting for you. *"Being confident of this very thing, that he which hath begun a good work in you will perform it until the day of Jesus Christ"* (Philippians 1:6).

When Jesus saw the man at the pool, He asked, *"Wilt thou be made whole?"* Notice, He did not say "healed," but "whole." Healing is surface-level; wholeness is deeper. *"But he was wounded for our transgressions, he was bruised for our iniquities: the chastisement of our peace was upon him; and with his stripes we are healed"* (Isaiah 53:5). Healing is promised, but wholeness is about restoration. After 38 years, this man needed a clean slate.

Then Jesus said, *"Rise, take up thy bed, and walk."* His words symbolized the man's responsibility to embrace his new life and leave behind past limitations. In our strength we are limited, but in God's strength there are no limits. His words call us to rise from spiritual paralysis, embrace our identity in Christ, and walk in freedom and purpose.

When you change your crowd, you change your narrative. So, if you are not walking, start while I am talking. A better you awaits, and better days are ahead.

Don't Dry Out

John 4:5-14
Then cometh he to a city of Samaria, which is called Sychar, near to the parcel of ground that Jacob gave to his son Joseph. Now Jacob's well was there. Jesus, therefore, being wearied with his journey, sat thus on the well: and it was about the sixth hour. There cometh a woman of Samaria to draw water: Jesus saith unto her, Give me to drink. (For his disciples were gone away unto the city to buy meat.) Then saith the woman of Samaria unto him, How is it that thou, being a Jew, askest drink of me, which am a woman of Samaria? For the Jews have no dealings with the Samaritans. Jesus answered and said unto her, If thou knewest the gift of God, and who it is that saith to thee, Give me to drink; thou wouldest have asked of him, and he would have given thee living water. The woman saith unto him, Sir, thou hast nothing to draw with, and the well is deep: from whence then hast thou that living water? Art thou greater than our father Jacob, which gave us the well, and drank thereof himself, and his children, and his cattle? Jesus answered and said unto her, Whosoever drinketh of this water shall thirst again: But whosoever drinketh of the water that I shall give him shall never thirst;

but the water that I shall give him shall be in him a well of water springing up into everlasting life.

You may have heard the phrase, "You don't miss your water until the well runs dry." This popular saying teaches us to value what we have while acknowledging the uncertainty of its longevity. Nothing that people of God have lasts forever. I've learned that people work harder in environments where appreciation is demonstrated early and often. I've witnessed individuals in circles where they've been depleted, deflated, defeated, and eventually deleted due to being taken advantage of by corrupt, insensitive, and selfish people.

What's been draining you? What are you involved in that leaves you ashy, brittle, itchy, parched, scaly, and withered? Do you find yourself wandering in the same wilderness you vowed never to return to? I am a kidney transplant recipient, so it's imperative that I have regular checkups. During one visit, I was surprised to hear I was dehydrated. As much water as I drink, I would never have thought a diagnosis of dehydration would apply to me. I've discovered that you can lack something vital and not even be aware of it. The tests and trials you endure will reveal if there's an insufficiency somewhere.

Have you crossed paths with someone who has dry lips, dry hands, dry eyes, dry feet, dry mouth, or a dry heart? These are signs of deficiency, an absence of something essential. I inquired whether I should increase my water intake or take a supplement. Instead, I was prescribed a hydration infusion, a four-hour procedure that delivered fluids intravenously. Paul shares in 2 Corinthians 4:16, *"For which cause we faint not; but though our outward man perish, yet the inward man is renewed day by day."*

It's frightening and frustrating to be around dry people: no passion, no smile, no energy, no pep, no ideas, no zeal, no emotion, no joy, no spunk, no praise. Always complaining. Always sad. Morbid. Depressed. Miserable. Just dry. Dryness can be contagious. My mother told me growing up, "Watch the company you keep!" Ironically, dryness can be found in the strangest places: the job, the club, the boardroom, the courtroom, the bar, the lounge, the PTA meeting, the family reunion, your household, the mall, and even the church.

May I tell you, "Wherever there's dryness, there's thirst!" Don't be fooled. Success or a smile does not mean there isn't a longing to be fulfilled. People all over the world are thirsty: thirsty for acceptance, access, accolades, affection, affirmation, and attention. Because of this thirst, you encounter people, or perhaps it is you, searching for arenas, avenues, opportunities, and outlets to quench this need. Matthew 5:6 declares, *"Blessed are they which do hunger and thirst after righteousness: for they shall be filled."*

No matter how much water you drink, regardless of your fluid intake, the real thirst is more than physical; it's spiritual. Paul writes in 1 Corinthians 15:46, *"Howbeit that was not first which is spiritual, but that which is natural; and afterward that which is spiritual."*

I call the book of John the "watery gospel" because of the numerous miracles involving water throughout its chapters. In chapter 2, Jesus turns water into wine. In chapter 5, Jesus heals the man at the pool of Bethesda after 38 years. In chapter 7, Jesus promises, *"Out of your belly shall flow rivers of living water."* In chapter 9, Jesus instructs the blind man to wash in the pool of Siloam. In chapter 11, Jesus weeps. In chapter 13, He washes His disciples' feet. In chapter 19, He says, *"I thirst"* on the cross. In chapter 21, He appears to His disciples at the Sea of Tiberias. I have often wondered how anyone could be thirsty with so much water around.

Jesus comes to Samaria. Samaria, meaning "watch" or "look out for," is near Sychar, meaning "drunk place," which contains a sacred parcel of land that Jacob left for his son Joseph, known as Jacob's well. Jesus sat at the well, weary from His journey, waiting for a divine encounter with a nameless woman from Samaria. Oftentimes, we believe we're waiting on God, but actually, God is waiting on us. I'm glad He waited. While I hesitated, procrastinated, was reluctant, skeptical, and undecided, Jesus waited on me! He strategically sent His disciples away to have one-on-one time with this woman.

My brothers and sisters, every now and then, it's good to be alone with Jesus. No TV. No social media. No children. No spouse. No distractions. Just you and Jesus. The hymnologist writes:

"I come to the garden alone,
While the dew is still on the roses;
And the voice I hear, falling on my ear,
The Son of God discloses.
And He walks with me, and He talks with me,
And He tells me I am His own,
And the joy we share as we tarry there,
None other has ever known."

He asks her for something to drink. She responds with a religious perspective, noting the disconnect between Jews and Samaritans. I've discovered that religion can sometimes get in the way of relationships. Religion can cause us to ponder doctrines, discerning what's true or false, but a solid relationship with God allows us to confidently say, *"I know my Redeemer lives!"* If you've been redeemed, declare it!

This dialogue between Jesus and the woman is fascinating. She mentions she has nothing to draw water with. So let me clarify: she comes to the well to get water but has no bucket, knowing the well is deep. How many times have we come to church where we can get fed, but we have no appetite? It's like taking an exam without a pencil. We are unprepared. We know all the gossip but have no gospel to spread. We have attitude but no gratitude. We're pretty but petty.

This woman had no intention of drawing water; she had other

agendas, motives, and plans. Many of us, beloved of God, come to His house with the wrong mindset, our hearts unfocused. We are empty rooms without furniture, asking people to sit down. We are unfinished and unfurnished. We never check our watches at parties. We don't worry about money on vacation. It's not an inconvenience when it's something we want to do.

We're thirsty, and we know it. We know we need water, but instead, we drink Moscato, rum and Coke, Apple Martinis, vodka, Gatorade, and Pepsi. Then we wonder why we're still thirsty. These drinks are costly. They intoxicate, leave you craving more, impair your body, damage your liver, cause diabetes, and only provide temporary satisfaction. Water is what you need. Water is free. It's on the house, with free refills.

When she saw Jesus, she realized He was unlike anyone she had met. He asked about her husband. Who are you connected to? Who's covering you? She admitted she had no husband. Jesus told her about the five husbands she had been married to and pointed out that the man she was currently dating wasn't hers. Many settle for Mr./Mrs. Right now when they cannot find Mr./Mrs. Right. Emotional emptiness follows multiple failed relationships. You're thirsty! Two side relationships, six baby mommas, a girlfriend, a fiancé. You're thirsty! Your life sounds like the 12 Days of Christmas, with a partridge in a pear tree. Your taste buds are off. Your palate is greedy. It's never enough.

Let me tell you: *"You can't continue to function like this!"* You're so dry, you can't even cry. You need water! Don't dry out in this season of life. You can't clean with a dry mop. You can't wash dishes with a dry sponge. You can't bathe without water. Water represents life. Water is refreshing. Water replenishes. Water may have no taste, but it touches the dry places in your life.

The Imprint of Certainty

St. John 20:24-29
Now Thomas, also known as Didymus, one of the Twelve, was not with the disciples when Jesus came. So the other disciples told him, "We have seen the Lord!" But he said to them, "Unless I see the nail marks in his hands and put my finger where the nails were, and put my hand into his side, I will not believe." A week later, his disciples were in the house again, and Thomas was with them. Though the doors were locked, Jesus came and stood among them and said, "Peace be with you!" Then he said to Thomas, "Put your finger here; see my hands. Reach out your hand and put it into my side. Stop doubting and believe."
Thomas said to him, "My Lord and my God!" Then Jesus told him, "Because you have seen me, you have believed; blessed are those who have not seen and yet have believed."

If you watch television regularly, you may have seen commercials for a company called 4Imprint. This business specializes in branding your logo on any merchandise of your choice, with a 4Imprint guarantee. The commercials depict scenarios where the outcome is uncertain: will the electricity be fixed for Monday Night Football? Is the doggy door the right size for Overseer? Can you unclog the toilet in time for Thanksgiving dinner? Each scenario ends with the customer asking, "Is the final result 4Imprint certain?" Ironically, this slogan sets the tone for what I want to discuss.

We are living in a season of uncertainty. Conversations with acquaintances, family, and friends often reveal that uncertainty dominates people's minds. Topics include politicians, financial stability, gun violence, health challenges, job security, social unrest, strikes, education, storms, vaccinations, and viruses. Each of these areas carries a shadow of uncertainty.

As the days pass, more people feel unsure about their future. To survive, hustling and coping mechanisms have entered the equation. "Robbing Peter to pay Paul" used to be a common strategy, but now Peter won't return your call, and Paul is tired of your excuses. Grandmaster Flash and the Furious Five said it well: *"Please don't push me, 'cause I'm close to the edge."* Have you been there? Are you there now? One foot on the edge and the other on a banana peel. 2 Corinthians 4 says we are "troubled on every side, perplexed, persecuted, and cast down," which reflects today's realities.

Beloved, I'm so grateful for my relationship with God, which helps me navigate my actions, emotions, and thoughts. Proverbs 3:5-6 declares, *"Trust in the LORD with all thine heart; and lean not unto thine own understanding. In all thy ways acknowledge him, and he shall direct thy paths."* If we're not careful, Satan will use our own actions, emotions, and thoughts as tools in his demonic workshop. My mother, Dr. Linda Moore, taught me as a child, "An idle mind is the devil's workshop, and boredom leads to sin." Now that I have three teenagers of my own, I understand the wisdom of her guidance. John 8:32 says, *"And ye shall know the truth, and the truth shall make you free."*

An idle mind is a breeding ground for negative consequences. Proverbs 16:27 states, *"Idle hands are the devil's work-*

shop; idle lips are his mouthpiece." Wicked thoughts can give birth to twins named Uncertainty and Iniquity. Psalms 66:18 warns, *"If I regard iniquity in my heart, the Lord will not hear me."* These twins make us walk a tightrope of turbulence. Faith and worry cannot coexist effectively. James 1:8 says, *"A double-minded man is unstable in all his ways."* Satan attacks both the heart and the mind, contaminating even good intentions. Romans 7:21 confirms, *"When I would do good, evil is always present."*

Boredom still exists, and it can be dangerous. Never lose the excitement of learning something new or taking on a challenge. Life is no longer a playground; it's a battlefield. Boredom can lead to sin. It can make you dial forbidden numbers or explore the unthinkable. Fatigue in the wrong place can be disastrous. Acts 20 recounts Eutychus, who fell asleep during Paul's preaching, tumbled from a third-story window, and died. His boredom made him vulnerable. This teaches us: *"When you're bored, watch out for the fall!"*

Paul avoided boredom by working hard to help others and meet the needs of the ministry. When you feel complacent, help someone else. While in Athens, Paul preached to anyone who would listen while waiting for Timothy and Silas. Galatians 6:9 motivates us: *"And let us not be weary in well doing: for in due season we shall reap if we faint not."*

Just as Missouri is called the "Show Me State," many people today want proof before believing. Social media and technology have made people skeptical. In this season of uncertainty, anxiety, discontentment, panic, restlessness, and worry rise. The enemy seeks to rob our peace, leaving us feeling trapped. 2 Timothy 1:7 says, *"For God hath not given us the spirit of fear; but of power, and of love, and of a sound mind."* God has brought us this far and will not leave us. God is! Declare to yourself, *"He never failed me yet!"*

Uncertainty allows doubt to creep in. Doubt makes you question your actions and revisit past decisions with regret. Romans warns us in chapter 14, *"He that doubteth is damned already."* Even Sarah laughed when told she would bear a child because doubt crept in despite years of prayer. Daniel's 21 days of petitions remind us that *"God heard you the first time."*

The spirit of doubt leads to desperation. Desperate times push people to desperate measures. Jada Pinkett's character, Stony, in *Set It Off* compromised herself to help her brother, only to find his acceptance to the school was false. Desperation can compromise morals, cause ill-advised borrowing, and lower expectations. Abraham and Sarah's scheme with Hagar illustrates the consequences of desperate actions. King Saul sought guidance from the witch of Endor. Be careful who you solicit help from when desperate; there are always costs attached. *"Watch your connections!"*

Jesus handpicked the twelve disciples, each with occupations, opposition, and purpose. Despite witnessing His miracles and receiving His love, the disciples were human. Peter denied Him, Judas betrayed Him, Thomas doubted Him. Humans are prone to uncertainty. *Romans 3* reminds us, *"For we have all sinned and come short of the glory of God."* Uncertainty plagued even powerful biblical figures like David, Elijah, and Jeremiah. Without God, we can do nothing. We are like ships without sails.

In our text, the disciples still coped with emotions after Jesus' death. Despite the resurrection, uncertainty about their future lingered. Conversations were likely filled with questions: Will He leave again? Will the Pharisees seek revenge? Uncertainty produces doubt, desperation, and distance from expectations. Ruth experienced uncertainty in three ways: famine, widowhood, and foreign lands. Her faith and loyalty to Naomi allowed God to provide Boaz, changing her life. Whatever you lose, don't lose your expectations. *"For it does not yet appear what it shall be."*

Thomas highlights the human need for certainty. Despite being a believer, he needed evidence of the resurrection: nail prints in Jesus' hands and wounds in His side. Words alone could not convince him. Often, we need personal proof because action speaks louder than words. Scripture repeatedly emphasizes the power of certainty.

Jesus, omniscient, knew Thomas' doubts and provided tangible evidence. Gideon's fleece in *Judges 6* illustrates God's accommodation of human need for confirmation. Thomas required a show-and-tell moment. Jesus presented the Imprint of His nails and wounds, proving the resurrection in living color.

Like Thomas, we often need personal encounters to restore confidence. Ask yourself, *"Are you imprint certain?"* Others' testimonies may not move your faith, but personal experience will. I can testify: five years since my kidney transplant, six months since lung surgery, five years in my own home, almost eight years at Zion Church, and 44 years of life without cancer. Jesus has shown me *"The Imprint of Certainty."* An imprint is a mark or outline on the body; I have seen His imprint in my life. I have walked with Him, and I am in awe of His goodness. I hope you are, too.

Again, I ask: *"Are you imprint certain?"* Surely goodness and mercy have followed me all the days of my life. If I had one word to describe Jesus, it would be: *Real!* So many doubt Him, but I cannot live without Him. He is that real to me.

The Celebration of Being Found

Luke 15:6, 9, 24
And when he cometh home, he calleth together his friends and neighbors, saying unto them, Rejoice with me; for I have found my sheep which was lost. And when she hath found it, she calleth her friends and her neighbors together, saying, Rejoice with me; for I have found the piece which I had lost. For this, my son was dead, and is alive again; he was lost, and is found. And they began to be merry.

NBC, also known as Channel 4, has introduced a series called *Found*, airing Thursdays at 10 pm. The show follows recovery specialist Gabi Mosely and her team as they locate missing people overlooked by media, law enforcement, and the public. Their work is personal because each team member has firsthand experience with a disappearance, whether it be themselves or a loved one. Gabi's methods push boundaries. She even enlists her childhood kidnapper to help the team while secretly keeping him in her basement. If you haven't seen it, I recommend adding it to your watchlist immediately.

Do you remember the best-kept secret place in school? Not

ICU

the cafeteria, gymnasium, science lab, art room, music room, or detention hall. No, it was the Lost and Found in the main office. Items left behind (mittens, hats, sneakers, notebooks, scarves, gym clothes, and even textbooks) were placed there. Sometimes you even find something better than what you originally lost.

Losing something at any age can be devastating. A family heirloom, a pet, glasses, keys, the TV remote, or a wallet. The search can be exhausting. We've accused our children or grandchildren of misplacing items, yelled through the house, or even forgotten where we put things. Sometimes we suspect guests of theft. As we grow older, we may become forgetful and overlook items sitting right in front of us. Searching everywhere, arguing, and feeling frustrated is universal.

Others are careful about lending things. A car, money, or jewelry may never be returned. Friendships strain over lost or unreturned items. Over time, I've learned: never give more than you're willing to lose. If the cost is too high, it's cheaper to hold on.

While losing something is frustrating, getting lost on a journey is another matter. Have you taken the wrong stop, followed incorrect directions, or missed a turn while driving? Everyone may know you're lost, but pride keeps you silent. Feeling lost, however, extends beyond physical directions. Life crossroads, circling patterns, and emotional or spiritual confusion create a sense of being lost. Proverbs 14:12 warns, *"There is a way which seemeth right unto a man, but the end thereof are the ways of death."* Feeling lost can place you in unfamiliar or dangerous circumstances. My mother reminded me daily, *"Never say never! Life can change in an instant."*

Luke, being a physician, offers a detailed account of Jesus as the ultimate physician and teacher. Jesus uses parables, which are simple stories conveying moral or spiritual truths. Parables use familiar situations to clarify deeper lessons. Proverbs 3:5 says, *"Trust in the LORD with all thine heart; and lean not unto thine own understanding."* Isaiah 55:8 reminds us, *"For my thoughts are not your thoughts, neither are your ways my ways, saith the LORD."* Proper understanding ensures effective Christian living and ministry.

In Luke 15, Jesus shares three parables centered on being lost. First is *The Lost Sheep*. Sheep wander, often chasing greener pastures. They can be dazed, distracted, and in need of guidance. The need for a Shepherd is revealed. John 10:11–16 illustrates the Good Shepherd: *"I am the good shepherd: the good shepherd giveth his life for the sheep. But he that is an hireling, and not the shepherd, whose own the sheep are not, seeth the wolf coming, and leaveth the sheep, and fleeth: and the wolf catcheth them, and scattereth the sheep. The hireling fleeth, because he is an hireling, and careth not for the sheep. I am the good shepherd, and know my sheep, and am known of mine. As the Father knoweth me, even so know I the Father: and I lay down my life for the sheep. And other sheep I have, which are not of this fold: them also I must bring, and they shall hear my voice; and there shall be one fold, and one shepherd."* The Good Shepherd is the guide, protector, healer, and overseer. A hireling works only for wages; the Shepherd works for the sheep's well-being.

Second is *The Lost Coin*. A woman loses one coin from a set of ten and searches diligently until she finds it. Have you ever felt lost in your own home? Overworked, underappreciated, overwhelmed? You can be present in church yet spiritually absent. Some attend out of habit, others for routine. *"Chatter will cause you to scatter!"* Loss of compassion, joy, love, spiritual appetite, and awareness can leave a vacant space. Filling it with the wrong things won't work; the peace of God is the only remedy. Matthew 17:27 illustrates God's provision: Peter catches a fish, and a coin inside pays his debt. God's work inside brings change on the outside.

Finally, *The Lost Son* portrays a father and two sons. The

youngest demands his inheritance and leaves prematurely. Gaining something too soon often leads to loss and regret. Quick-rich schemes, premature decisions, and immaturity can leave you holding the bag of consequences. All three parables begin with loss and end in recovery. Cried, moaned, prayed, searched, and ultimately found the Lord.

My celebration of being found continues today. Jesus has restored me from brokenness, abandonment, failure, abuse, barrenness, heartbreak, and grief. I came to Him weary, worn, and sad. He became my resting place, and I am glad. Rejoice!

Rejoicing In Rejection

Luke 2:7
And she brought forth her firstborn son, and wrapped him in swaddling clothes, and laid him in a manger; because there was no room for them in the inn.

Christmas comes every year. Individuals journey throughout the world to get their last-minute shopping done. Trees are decorated. Houses and streets are full of lights. Carolers are singing. Parties are being celebrated on the job. The radio, the internet, and the television have our attention as they advertise various ways to promote this holiday. This is indeed the most wonderful time of the year.

Unfortunately, with all of this holly and all this jolly, Santa Claus has redirected, rejected, and replaced the true reason for the season. Some even call this season X-Mas because they have X Christ out of the equation. Some don't believe in Christmas; they observe Kwanzaa. Those of the Jewish faith don't believe in Christmas because it's a Christian holiday, so they observe Hanukkah. There are so many options that are offered about religion. Catholics believe one thing, Muslims believe another, and the Five Percenters believe something else, but I'll take Jesus for mine. Christmas is not a time to exclude Jesus. If we ever needed the Lord before, we sure do need Him now. Proverbs 3:6 shares, *"In all thy ways acknowledge him, And he shall direct thy paths."* Tell your neighbor, "I believe God!"

Every year during the Christmas season, I reread the Christmas story over and over again. No matter how often you read a story, there are always new treasures hidden that, with a spiritual search, will be discovered. Matthew and Luke are the only two gospels that give us an inside look at the birth of Jesus Christ. In the Old Testament, He's Christ concealed, and in the New Testament, He's Christ revealed. I want to encourage you to rejoice in rejection!

It is easy to rejoice in acceptance. It is easier to rejoice in inclusion. The words rejoice and rejection aren't two expressions you often hear together. Peanut butter and jelly. Bacon and eggs. Breakfast, lunch, and dinner. Liver and onions. These are all phrases we can digest because they seem to mesh, but rejoicing and rejection live on opposite sides of town.

Have you ever been rejected? Told no? Got overlooked? Told you weren't good enough? Someone else being selected over you, even though you were the more qualified candidate? Cut from a team. Not acceptable to the college of your choice. Rejection is a hard pill to swallow. It can leave bitterness in your heart and in your mouth. Rejection can birth low self-esteem, a lack of confidence, and cripple a person from ever trying, applying, or striving again. Rejection is often difficult to describe. Trust me when I tell you, it's one of the most horrible and terrible feelings an individual can encounter.

Many of us in this Christmas season have mixed emotions. In our travels, we witness families enjoying each other's company. Husbands with wives. Mommies with daughters. Fathers with sons. These scenes only open up the wounds of the disconnect we have with our loved ones who have rejected us. Many haven't received an invitation to Christmas dinner. Fathers who won't claim children. Mothers so preoccupied that they don't acknowledge their own kids. Spouses who function like strangers in the night. The relationships with relatives can go left at any moment, all because of the unspoken feelings of rejection.

After you've extended your love, time, heart, finances, body, and soul to an individual, only to hear they're moving on to someone else who just came along or just might have been there the whole time, it can shake your entire core. I know they told you, "It's me, not you," but you can't ignore the voices in the back of your mind that maybe the real problem is you. Rejection has a way of making you think that the issue is you. Something is wrong with you. It can make you doubt and second-guess yourself.

So, as you're sitting under the sound of my voice, you might be struggling with the ghosts of grief because, in your mind, you saw things turning out another way. Perhaps you enrolled in school to pursue a career, hours of classes, months of papers, and years of studying, only to be denied a job because there are no openings right now. "Don't call us; we'll call you!" It's enough to take your breath away. Rejection can leave you speechless. So, holidays aren't the greatest times for you. You might not even have a tree up this year, and if you do, all that's under it are memories of rejection because your son won't even call you back. Your daughter is married and won't let you see your grand-kids. So, you're left thinking what everyone else is doing, who cooked, or what games are being played, because you've been purposefully excluded from the family gatherings.

As I was writing this, something unusual happened. I believe there's always a spiritual application that can be applied to a natural situation. In the last few days, I've noticed that my dog, Overseer, has been adamant about closed doors. He gets ferocious and growls when someone begins to close the door. Maybe it's because there are times when everyone in the house retreats to their own quarters and closes the door on him, leaving him in the hallway.

We all need some personal time. With all of the demands of life that are stressing and stretching us, we yearn for some personal space. Some of us, beloved, aren't fortunate enough to still get away. So we go to the gym, go to a diner, go for a walk, go to Starbucks, or even sit in our car just to find a moment of silence. When the door is closed, Overseer moans, whines, barks, and scratches until one of us opens the door and lets him in.

The Holy Ghost showed me, if a dog is not a fan of the door being closed on him, and this is his reaction, how do we respond when doors are closed on us? We get mad, angry, frustrated, annoyed, and aggravated, too. It's something about a door being closed on us while there is activity on the other side that we're not included in that screams rejection. A closed door, dear friends, ignites a closed me. I'm malfunctioning. I'm shutting down. I'm numb. I don't talk; I won't open up. I'm as cold as ice. I'm isolated. I'm a loner. I keep to myself. I constantly wrestle because the silence is so loud it seems like an echo in a concert of all the other times I've ever been rejected.

I know I may have asked you earlier, but I just need to ask again, "Have you ever been rejected?" Rejected from a fraternity. Rejected from a sorority. Rejected from society. The episode of rejection is being rehearsed in many areas of our lives. It's unbelievable, it's unbearable, it's unimaginable. It's a painful prison. It can make one commit homicide or suicide. If you don't believe me, ask Taraji P. Henson, who starred in *Acrimony*. Her rage erupted from the perspective that she felt rejected and that someone else was living her dream life, living in her dream house with the man of her dreams. When your dreams fall apart, you are actually watching the death of everything you have ever envisioned. Rejection can transform all your dreams into a nightmare. Unexplained dreams symbolize the existence of unresolved issues.

You may ask, "How do I know so much about rejection?" I'm well acquainted with rejection since you asked. Can I be completely transparent with you? My biological father rejected me from the moment I was born, never publicly acknowledging me, leaving me to question privately, "Why he don't want me?" Growing up, I wondered, wandered, and worried if I would ever be good enough to get the acceptance I desperately craved. Craving, carrying, and crying. The weight of rejection was definitely a huge load on such small shoulders.

Don't get me wrong, I'm forever appreciative, grateful, and thankful for all my mother, Dr. Linda Moore, sacrificed to create an amazing environment, outstanding upbringing, and incredible foundation for me. There were still times when I felt empty, though I was surrounded with everything. Rejection can take a piece out of you every day. I faced rejection by girls who I liked, who didn't like me, who teased me about my ears, my nose, and my lips, and who were more attracted to athletes than to a boy in the chorus.

Then, to think that finally my father would be proud of me, when he vowed to come to my graduation and never showed up. Excuses after excuses about why he wasn't present at my trial sermon, ordinations, installations, proclamations, and consecrations. Then, to make matters worse, he didn't bother to show up to my wedding or come to his grandchildren's christenings and dedications. Rejected by churches that gave me opportunities, only to learn later they were using my talents, gifts, and prostituting my anointing to advance their agenda. Hope dashed. Expectations crushed.

I've even been rejected in pastoring. Investments unappreciated. Money loaned. Funerals preached for individuals who weren't even members. Time away from my family to counsel their families. Then folks suddenly leave you high and dry. Ignore you, don't speak to you, or act like you don't exist. Don't return your call. Walk away without a call. Abandon their positions. Don't value a face-to-face conversation, just send you a text: "I won't be back!" Post about you. Sub about you. Telling their side of the story of how they were victimized/abused, never mentioning how they were beneficiaries.

So, what do you do? Just shake your head and try to shake off the reality of not being wanted. So, as I strive to continue giving, singing, training, preaching, teaching, dancing, and serving with a broken heart, knowing there's someone who still values what God has instilled in me to share, with the promise that Jesus remembers when others forget. In my meditation, I remembered the words of the Apostle Paul to the Galatian church, *"And let us not be weary in well doing: for in due season we shall reap, if we faint not."*

I suppose why this text in Luke 2:7 is so intriguing to me is because Mary and Joseph, after traveling such a long distance, have to hear that there's no room in the inn. Can you imagine a virgin girl, who didn't ask for any of this, is on a barren road, nine months pregnant, looking for a place to have a baby? Accompanied by a man who is searching for answers and seeking solutions to handle all this, and now you are faced with rejection.

What do you mean, "There's no room!"? What am I gonna tell a woman who's been sitting on a donkey for seven days, who's crying, cramping, complaining, and carrying, that there's no room? Her water can break at any moment, and rejection is the last thing she needs to hear. After you've pulled, pushed, and pressed to overcome these obstacles, who wants to have to deal with the consequences of having no room? I'm desperate. I'm out of options. I'm overwhelmed. I've got some good news for you: "God is making room for you!"

After all of the rejection Mary and Joseph endured, after the countless attempts to discourage the plan of God, after you faced rejection after rejection, you came across a spot that was reserved just for you. No prior notice, just confirmation that you're in the right place at the right time. God has a place for you. It might not be a mansion, it might not be a condo or a loft, but it's mine. It's not what I pictured. It didn't include who I thought it would be. It's not where I imagined it would be. I can take a load off. I can put my feet up.

Most importantly, it's a good place to have a baby. Mary conceived Jesus in a manger. I'm out of ICU. I'm out of critical condition. I'm out of surgery.

The story of my life: Jesus grew up rejected by men and women. Rejected by his brothers. Rejected by his disciples. Even rejected by the crowd, who chose a murderer named Barabbas over Him. Isaiah declares, *"He is despised and rejected of men; a man of sorrows, and acquainted with grief."* David echoes those same sentiments, describing Jesus as *"the stone that builders rejected."* *"Foxes have holes, and birds of the air have nests."* Sounds like rejection to me.

Those who have been through a series of rejections, I've got a reason to rejoice because He was born to deliver me, and He died to save me. It's been a rough road and a tough process. I've discovered every rejection was followed by God's direction. He directed me to the right job, the right companion, the right house, and the right church. What's the matter with Jesus? "He's alright!"

Despite everyone who walked away, I've got a Savior who stepped in, made me feel wanted, wrapped His arms around me, and loved me unconditionally. Storm clouds may rise. Strong winds may blow. I found a Savior, and He's sweet, I know. Now, I'm proud to say without hesitation, "You can't make me doubt Him, I know too much about Him!" Rejoice in the Lord always, and again I say rejoice. Years and years of rejection only make room for rejoicing. Your days ahead are going to be bigger, better, brighter, and greater.

'Tis The Season For A Pep Talk

1 Samuel 30:1-6
And it came to pass, when David and his men were come to Ziklag on the third day, that the Amalekites had invaded the south, and Ziklag, and smitten Ziklag, and burned it with fire; And had taken the women captives that were therein: they slew not any, either great or small, but carried them away, and went on their way. So David and his men came to the city, and behold, it was burned with fire; and their wives, and their sons, and their daughters, were taken captives. Then David and the people that were with him lifted up their voice and wept, until they had no more power to weep. And David's two wives were taken captives, Ahinoam the Jezreelitess, and Abigail the wife of Nabal the Carmelite. And David was greatly distressed; for the people spake of stoning him, because the soul of all the people was grieved, every man for his sons and for his daughters: but David encouraged himself in the Lord his God.

We all have a moment when we talk to ourselves. Quite possibly, you were thinking out loud, contemplating something in your mind, and had to reason within yourself about how to resolve the matter at hand. Now, don't get me wrong, talking to yourself isn't the problem because there are occasions when talking to yourself will be the difference between sinking and swimming in the restless sea of tides.

The issue arises when answering yourself, especially when you start responding to the inner voices in your head. Have you ever had to cope with voices in your head? If Satan can talk angels out of Heaven, surely he can talk you into Hell. Be mindful of the voices you listen to. Let's go a little further: how about managing the noise not just on the inside, but on the outside as well? Isaiah 26:3 *declares, "Thou wilt keep him in perfect peace, whose mind is stayed on thee."*

I've shared this golden nugget with my congregation in the past, and I believe in this season it bears repeating: *"Man will miss Heaven by 18 inches!"* That is the distance between your head and your heart. These two vital parts of the human anatomy are under daily stress. Heart palpitations, migraines, and high blood pressure are symptoms that result from stress in those areas.

The Apostle Paul in 2 Corinthians 4 uses words like troubled, perplexed, persecuted, and cast down. Why? While my mind is navigating decisions and dilemmas, my heart is negotiating facts and feelings. John 14:1 *shares, "Let not your heart be troubled."* The songwriter sums 2024 up for us: *"Trouble in my way, I had to cry sometimes. I laid awake at night, but that's all right, Jesus will fix it after a while."*

This crowded world can often seem like a place of isolation. I know the pandemic is a conversation of the past, but there are still a few individuals who are still living life in quarantine. You believe distance, being standoffish, or even a level of shadiness is the answer. Don't be fooled by the people you follow or who follow you on social media platforms, because their reach will never reach you when it matters the most.

There's an African American spiritual, "Sometimes I Feel Like a Motherless Child," that expresses the pain and despair of separation one may experience being apart from family and friends. In this scenario, the composer details them as being a long way from home. Sadly, our support systems can be so close, yet so far. Who should be there isn't. Who you don't want to be is trying to be. Folks' agendas and motives are often under a microscope.

The difficulty I'm currently battling is that I'm actually left to deal with all of this by myself. Have you ever felt alone? Nobody cares. Nobody understands. Abandoned. Forsaken. Rejected. You're left with a plethora of baggage that no one is available to help you carry. That's why the airline has a limit on how much baggage a passenger can take on board. Most airlines will allow you to check one bag and have one carry-on bag. There is normally a maximum weight limit of 50 pounds per checked bag, as well as a size restriction. Oversized and overweight cargo comes with a price.

Some of us are violating the baggage policy because we constantly attempt to overload the arenas of our hearts and our minds with overanalyzing and overthinking. Hebrews 12:1 *reminds us to "Lay aside every weight and the sin which so easily beset us."* You need to thank God for baggage claim. Baggage claim is the section in an airport where arriving passengers collect luggage that has been carried in the bottom of the aircraft. Every now and then, we need to turn those heavy loads over to the Lord and leave them there so we can get to our desired destination.

While we're traveling, God will give us a first-class service of new strength, and we'll testify, *"I feel better, so much better, since I laid my burdens down!"* There are a few occasions when the airline loses your luggage. I believe God has a way of eliminating what's not necessary. He knows what you need and what you don't need. If you know God is subtracting the strain in your situation, give Him praise and scream, *"Lord, do it for me right now!"*

The book of 1 Samuel tells the story of the fall of one king and the rise of another king. Proverbs 16:18 *states, "Pride goeth before destruction, and a haughty spirit before a fall."* The phrase *"Pride goeth before a fall"* means that when someone is excessively arrogant or proud, they are likely to experience a downfall or failure. Not heeding warnings against overconfidence and boasting can lead to negative consequences.

Solomon adds to the equation: *"A haughty spirit"* is an individual who acts superior and looks down on others. The legendary gospel artists, the Jackson Southernaires, told us through the song, *"Don't Look Down on a Man Unless You're Picking Him Up!"* I've learned that you can be overconfident in one area and lack confidence in another area. You can be successful with advice for someone else's children, and that same advice proves to be unsuccessful in your own household. You can be solid in test-taking and fearful of interviews.

Some leaders use authority to mask their own insecurities. King Herod, King Nebuchadnezzar, and King Saul were examples of allowing power to go to their head. The Bible notes how these men were ultimately removed because of their abuse of power. God knows how to bring you down to size. I've discovered folks out here are trying to be big, but the sad part is, little got 'em. Ralph Kramden said, *"Be careful how you treat people on the up because you'll meet the same people on the way down!"*

Paul confesses to the church at Corinth, which is good for the soul: *"And lest I should be exalted above measure through the abundance of the revelations, there was given to me a thorn in the flesh, the messenger of Satan to buffet me, lest I should be exalted above measure."* Matthew 23:12 *echoes these same sentiments, "And whosoever shall exalt himself shall be humbled: and he that shall humble himself shall be exalted."*

Luke 14:11 *adds, "All who lift themselves up will be brought low, and those who make themselves low will be lifted up."*

You recall what Michelle Obama told us: *"When they go low, we go high!"* High-five your neighbor and tell them, *"Being humble will take you higher!"*

A young boy named David replaces King Saul by being in the right place at the right time. God took him from the back burner to the head of the table. From keeping sheep to slaying giants. From being overlooked to being the center of attention. Won't God do it? Let me encourage you: when God says it's your time, it's your time. *"The first shall be last, and the last shall be first!"*

"The first" are the privileged, prestigious, and selfish who get ahead in this life while defying God's commandments. They will receive condemnation in the life to come. "The last," though rejected by the world, will receive a great reward in heaven. *Psalms 37 notes, "Fret not thyself because of evildoers, neither be thou envious against the workers of iniquity. For they shall soon be cut down like the grass, and wither as the green herb."*

David, being king, has the responsibility of leading men. One can't effectively lead until they faithfully learn how to follow. His journey leads him to a myriad of places, but in our text, they land in Ziklag. Ziklag was a place of refuge and strategy for David and his faithful followers. If you're going to be great in God and desire to develop spiritually, you'll have to take a trip to Ziklag because it reveals what you're made of. In addition, it discloses what's on the inside of you. Whatever is on the inside of you, no matter how hard you try to suppress it, is going to come out. Whether it's jealousy, envy, character, or genuineness, scream: *"It's coming out!"*

Ziklag reveals and discloses because, in Hebrew, it means *"pressed down."* Olives that are pressed produce oil. Grapes that are pressed produce wine. What are you producing when you get pressed? What happens when your buttons are pressed? How much weight can you bench press? How are you handling the crowds and the circus clowns? How are you reacting to the lions and liars in the jungle? These are conversations that are long overdue. Your responses speak volumes. Tell God, *"I'm ready to talk about it!"*

When David and his men came to Ziklag back from the battlefield, they found it destroyed by fire, and their wives, sons, and daughters were taken captive. So, David and his men wept aloud until they had no strength left to cry. The story of my life can be summed up in two words: affections and afflictions. Whatever I've put my heart into, Satan found a way to break it into a million pieces: job, family, church, relationships. I've always seemed left holding the bag with a shattered heart. The one and only place I had security and stability was destroyed.

I finally have to be honest: *"I have no more strength to cry!"* Many of us are just shells of ourselves because, at this point, we're numb. I know some of y'all are trying not to cry. The Holy Ghost has released us this morning to go on and cry! I'm not crying just about what I lost, but who I lost. I have to be completely transparent. I lost some things, but more importantly, I lost someone valuable, expensive, rare, precious, priceless. Who was it? ME! I lost myself trying to be everything to everybody, trying to make up for what I never had, trying to fill the gaps, the space, the voids that others never had. In all of this pleasing people, I lost me!

After those who were dealt a bad hand took into account what they lost, they decided to stone, persecute, and scandalize the only person who was there for them: ME! *"I'm so tired of others taking out their unhappiness on me!"*

David identifies this grievance. Nobody understands the struggle he faced with his father, Jesse, the sullied reputation of his mother, the tug of war for acceptance from his brothers, and his survival amid the attacks and threats from Saul. Now his own men, who fought for and secured victory with him, are against him too. Let's not forget his wives and daughters were among those taken captive. David was being stretched in all kinds of directions. What do you do when you're stretched? What do you do when you've run out of solutions?

David's resilience was demonstrated in the rubble of Ziklag. In the past, he would have talked to Jonathan. He was used to talking to the sheep as he tended to his father's flock. He often talked to Samuel for advice and guidance. Those you may have talked to in these seasons might be overwhelmed, preoccupied, or even transitioned. Today, you must stop talking about it, searching for individuals to hear your plight, and talk to yourself. David encouraged himself in the Lord. *"I'm an overcomer! I'm more than a conqueror! I am fearfully and wonderfully made! I am what God says I am! I am the head and not the tail! Above and not beneath! The lender and not the borrower! I'm better than this! I can't quit! I won't throw in the towel! This too shall pass!"*

'Tis the season for a pep talk! It's a much-needed talk intended to make someone feel more equipped to charge ahead in discouraging situations, an opportunity to increase one's moral awareness, and a discourse designed to awaken the champion inside, especially when feeling defeated. It's imperative for you to *"Leave it alone! Resist the urge for revenge, let God fight your enemies! Resist the temptation to indulge in sin! Get away from me, Satan, I'm God's property!"* Talk yourself out of depression and dependency. Talk yourself into the belief that it won't always be like this. Lay your hands on yourself and tell yourself, *"I'm going to make it!"*

I must tell Jesus all of my troubles. I cannot bear these burdens alone in my distress. He will kindly aid me. Jesus can help me. Jesus alone. Have a little talk with Jesus. Tell Him all about your trouble. He'll hear your faintest cry, and He'll answer by and by. Then you'll feel the prayer wheel turning and know the fire is burning. If you have a little talk with Jesus, He'll make it all right. Don't ever give up!

Ziklag is not your final resting place; it is only the test of kings and queens. Encourage yourself in the Lord, pursue, recover, and move forward. Lastly, stop telling your problems to God and start telling your problems about your God.

I've Been Rocked, But I'm Still Rolling

Acts 14:19-20
And there came thither certain Jews from Antioch and Iconium, who persuaded the people, and having stoned Paul, drew him out of the city, supposing he had been dead. Howbeit, as the disciples stood round about him, he rose up, and came into the city: and the next day he departed with Barnabas to Derbe.

Time is indeed moving swiftly. One day we're saying, "Happy New Year," and the next it seems like we're getting ready for Thanksgiving and Christmas. As the seconds turn to minutes, minutes turn to hours, hours turn into days, days turn to weeks, weeks turn to months, and months turn to years. I discovered we're all marching in a parade called life. Life can be difficult. Whether you've been in church all your life or just came to church for the first time today, life can be difficult. Whether you're saved, sanctified, Holy Ghost-filled, fire-baptized, or a jive turkey, life can be difficult. It can be so difficult that doubt and uncertainty can cause even the steadiest to question their judgment and their next move.

The devil's agenda has been made crystal clear. It's deliberate, forthcoming, and premeditated. Job 1:7 confirms, *"And the LORD said unto Satan, Whence comest thou? Then Satan answered the LORD, and said, From going to and fro in the earth, and from walking up and down in it."* John 10:10a reinforces, *"The thief cometh not, but for to steal, and to kill, and to destroy."* With us fully aware of Satan's plans and plots, our responsibility is to be diligent about our destiny, intelligent about our integrity, and vigilant about our victory. *Jesus declares, "I am come that they might have life, and that they might have it more abundantly."*

Each year comes with its own set of trials and tribulations. Our New Year's resolutions have become resentful in a matter of moments. Your expectations have quickly evaporated. Dreams turned into nightmares. These disasters at your doorstep have been designed to knock you off your feet. Psalms 1:3 writes, *"And he shall be like a tree planted by the rivers of water."* The old saying, "wheebles wobble, but they don't fall down." I survived every liar and every lion. I survived what others succumbed to. I even survived what some might consider near-death situations. Isaiah 54:17 declares, *"No weapon that is formed against thee shall prosper."*

Life is indeed a rollercoaster ride of unexplainable and unexpected twists and turns that are flooded with a never-dull-moment narrative. The character highlighted this morning is well-versed in these never-ending episodes and events. The books of Acts focus on the Apostle Paul's journey of conversion and conviction. Saul was a persecutor of the church. We're all familiar with the persecution of the church. People have opinions about the church. Some believe the church is a hoax and a hustle. Some believe our gospel ambassadors are counterfeit and fraudulent. Others believe the church is filled with hatred and hypocrisy. Matthew 16:18 shares, *"And I say also unto thee, That thou art Peter, and upon this rock I will build my church; and the gates of hell shall not prevail against it."* It didn't say it wouldn't assail; it said it wouldn't prevail. Can you confess, "Church kept me safe, sane, and saved"? I went to church one night, and my heart wasn't right, but something got a hold of me. COVID tried to keep me shut out, but how many remember the old-fashioned church shut-in where we prayed and prayed until I found the Lord.

The transformation of this mercenary to missionary only proves that not only does life involve us, but it evolves us. 2 Corinthians 5:17 records, *"Therefore if any man be in Christ, he is a new creature: old things are passed away; behold, all things are become new."* Look at my hands. They look new. Look at my feet. They did too. The things I used to do, I don't do anymore, and the places I used to go, I don't go anymore. A wonderful change has come over you. Anytime you decide to make changes, both opportunities and opposition will arise. This encounter on the Damascus Road was breaking news and became barbershop, hairdresser, and nail salon talk that rocked the Jewish community. The text that arrests our attention finds Paul as the common denominator in the conflict between the Jews of Antioch and Iconium. Isn't it amazing how enemies can call a temporary truce with each other and readjust their scope on you? Encourage yourself and say, "God is turning this setback into a comeback!"

I got too close; Paul now has all eyes on him. The spotlight is bigger and brighter, but not better. The people have been persuaded to stone him. You have been "Been Rocked, but You're Still Rolling." Stoning is well-documented in the Holy Writ. You recall the woman caught in adultery. The Pharisees wanted to persuade Jesus to enforce the law of having her stoned to death. Jesus, being an attorney who was astute and possessed tremendous acumen, was more clever than Matlock, sharper than Perry Mason, wiser than Johnny Cochran. Jesus decided to use the ground as a blackboard and teach the Pharisees grace and mercy. Class was in session when He wrote on the ground, *"He without sin, let them cast the first stone."* Jesus set the woman free from her accusers and told her to roll. Tell somebody, "You may have stones, but I've got a rock."

As I head back to the Bronx, when they stoned Paul, supposing he was dead, they dragged him out of the city. He arose and came back the next day. I might seem lifeless. I've been pushed to the limit. I've experienced life-changing circumstances, but high-five ten people and tell them, "There's still some life left in me!"

Bereavement rocked me, sickness rocked me, unemployment rocked me, and the pandemic rocked me. I left a good job in the city working for the man every night and day, and I never lost one minute of sleep. I was worrying 'bout the way the things might've been, you know that big wheel keeps on turning, Proud Mary keeps on burning, and we're rolling, rolling, rolling, rolling on the river.

Withdrawals and Deposits

Job 1:2-5; 42:12
And there were born unto him seven sons and three daughters. His substance also was seven thousand sheep, and three thousand camels, and five hundred yoke of oxen, and five hundred she asses, and a very great household; so that this man was the greatest of all the men of the east. And his sons went and feasted in their houses, every one his day; and sent and called for their three sisters to eat and to drink with them. And it was so, when the days of their feasting were gone about, that Job sent and sanctified them, and rose up early in the morning, and offered burnt offerings according to the number of them all: for Job said, It may be that my sons have sinned, and cursed God in their hearts. Thus did Job continually. So the Lord blessed the latter end of Job more than his beginning: for he had fourteen thousand sheep, and six thousand camels, and a thousand yoke of oxen, and a thousand she asses.

Ever since God formed man in the Garden of Eden with the dust of the ground, man has been making deposits in the earth realm. It was man's mandate from the very beginning to be fruitful and multiply so the earth could be replenished. In order to properly till the ground, seed must be planted for a harvest to grow. The responsibility of man was great, as God entrusted him with dominion over all the creatures on the land and in the sea.

As time evolved, another deposit was made as man now embraced the calling of fatherhood. Good fathers don't just leave an inheritance for their children, but also provide for their families, protect their families, and prepare their families for the future. There is another level of security a father brings when his presence is felt in the home that makes those in the house feel safer and sleep better. Nobody will ever know the daily demand on fathers to do all that is necessary so their children can be well taken care of. Over time, time and a half, extra shifts, perhaps even a second job, may be needed to cover the needs of the family. If you check the father's account, you'll discover numerous transactions that are processed to be sure there's meat in the barrel and money in the bank. On this day, the sacrifice of a father often gets overlooked because many enjoy what he puts on the table, and do not celebrate what he brings to the table. Sometimes folk just enjoy your deposits without taking into account the depth, the details, and the desperation a father is tasked to maintain all that has been given to his charge.

For decades, television has depicted different types of fathers. Andy Taylor, Greg Brady, Ward Cleaver, Rob Petrie, and Archie Bunker were all white men who had good professions to support their families. On the other hand, James Evans, Fred Sanford, Carl Winslow, Phillip Banks, George Jefferson, and Lester Jenkins were all black men who struggled to provide for their families. Dr. Heathcliff Huxtable arguably was the exception to the rule because of his successful practice as an obstetrician, and his wife, Claire, being a partner at a law firm certainly eased the financial load in the household.

Fatherhood in every sense of the word is challenging, and in no way am I being biased, but I believe when it comes to black fathers, there's some additional pressure from society to be successful. Men are often so burdened with the business of keeping the account from going into a negative balance that the diligence of how they manage the balance, the act of family and finances, is usually neglected.

Have you ever been in a place where things just don't add up? *James 1* reminds us to *"count it all joy,"* but as you count it all too many times, you've discovered you've been shortchanged. In other words, the deposits are noticed, but the withdrawals are unnoticed. Have you asked yourself, "When are my investments going to pay off?" Too many withdrawals and no deposits will print out a receipt that reads "insufficient funds." I want to highlight some accounts involving fathers in the Holy Writ.

Noah was commanded by God to build an ark because it was going to rain, not the chances of rain like we hear the meteorologist predict, but God was indeed sending a flood that would wash humanity off the face of the earth due to their lack of obedience and sinful behavior. You may have gotten caught in the rain a few times, but the flood missed you. You and I have both done enough to be wiped out, eliminated, and cut off, but since you're alive, I know that you weren't lucky; you've been spared.

There were specific instructions given to Noah of the length, width, and height of the ark, but also to include every animal two by two, along with the safety of his wife, his three sons, and their wives. The problem we have in this present day is that we try to take everyone on board, then wonder why the ship is sinking. You recall Abraham told his servants to stay down at the bottom of the mountain while he and his son, Isaac, went yonder to worship. Some people God removes from your life not to isolate you, but to protect you. Let them go. It will be better for you.

Noah, praising God for his survival, planted a vineyard and drank wine, which left him drunk and exposed. Ham saw his father uncovered. Sadly, instead of covering him, like he's always been covered, he chose to expose him to his other two brothers. The two brothers, Japheth and Shem, walked in backwards with a garment, so they would maintain their honor and respect for their father. What a horrible thing to have your child expose your deficiencies, expose your faults, or dishonor you in moments of weakness. This kind of violation certainly takes a piece out of you. Brothers and sisters, this isn't a deposit; it's a withdrawal that can leave you emotionally, physically, and mentally damaged.

Isaac had grown old, and his vision had become dim. In that vulnerable position, his younger son, Jacob, with the help of his mother, Rebecca, hatched a scheme to get her husband, Isaac, to bless Jacob instead of their older son, Esau. Using animal skins and blood, Jacob went into his father's quarters. Even though Isaac was blind, his other four senses were heightened. Both his hearing and his touch came into the picture: *"You sound like Jacob, but you feel like Esau."* What a sad state of affairs to deceive a man who now can't see, who's been looking out for you your whole life. You might not have 20/20 vision, but God has a way of showing you who people really are.

The iconic poet and writer, Maya Angelou, said, *"When folks show you who they are, believe them."* How many episodes do you have to watch to know that everyone can't be trusted? Don't ask me to trust you when I'm still spitting up water from the last time you almost let me drown. *"For the arms of flesh will fail you."* Sometimes, our greatest pain comes from folk closest to us, and even more alarming, they might be in our own house. I would love to get a good night's sleep, but how can I when I'm sleeping with the enemy? Can I make a confession? I've been stabbed, but when I saw who was holding the knife, I lost it. You have to be mindful of those who will strike in your time of weakness.

Let me remind you to *"Watch the company you keep!"* The old adage offers, *"Familiarity breeds contempt."* Contempt in any relationship often arises from unhealed conflict, unfulfilled emotional needs, a lack of empathy, and a sense of feeling unappreciated or unacknowledged. It can manifest as sarcasm, mockery, dismissive language, or nonverbal communication like eyerolling or stares of intimidation. Deep down, it's rooted in a feeling of jealousy and the comfort that boundaries no longer exist.

The Psalmist summed it up perfectly: *"Yea, mine own familiar friend, in whom I trusted, Which did eat of my bread, hath lifted up his heel against me."* This kind of deception is not a deposit; it's a withdrawal that leaves you questioning your surroundings. Ecclesiastes 3:4 notes, *"a time to weep, and a time to laugh; a time to mourn, and a time to dance."* As we consider David, this verse certainly describes the experiences of the grief and glory of fatherhood.

Yes, David was a man after God's own heart. The courageous warrior who fought the bear, the lion, and the wolves, all to protect his father's sheep. Oh my! The undisputed champion that was victorious over the undefeated Philistine, Goliath, with a slingshot and five smooth stones, which led to the unforgettable chant from the crowd: *"Saul killed his thousands, but David slayed his ten thousands."* A relieved king who danced out of his clothes because the Ark of the Covenant was safely back in Israel.

While we highlight these moments of success, let's not forget to add to his extensive resume moments of sadness. David had to cope with the death of the child he shared with Bathsheba, the wife of his loyal servant, Uriah. This is a prime example of the negative consequences associated with sinful acts. Romans 6:23 reminds us, *"For the wages of sin is death."* It's extremely difficult to deal with any type of bereavement, but especially burying your own children. Usually, the main focus is on the mother's agony, but let's not ignore the toll it takes on the fathers as well. I've heard various accounts that when children die, a part of you dies too. When it's your turn to go through, that season is filled with both turbulence and turmoil. In other words, when it rains, it pours.

David, on another occasion, faces two different sides of the spectrum concerning his daughter, Tamar, and his son, Absalom. When Tamar was set up by men in the king's court, she was ultimately raped by her half-brother, Ammon. When Tamar shared with her brother Absalom about the horrific encounter, he waited two years before he avenged his sister's assault, but he finally had Ammon killed. Later, Absalom led a revolt against his father by usurping King David's authority among the soldiers. This act of rebellion led to his own demise when Absalom's long flowing hair got caught on a tree, causing his neck to be broken. Pass this down your row: *"Don't get hung up by your hang-ups!"* This type of betrayal can leave a bitter taste and the weight of withdrawal on any person.

I've gone through some accounts involving fathers in the Old Testament; it's only appropriate that we briefly examine the fathers in the New Testament so this message can come full circle. A frustrated father named Jairus, whose 12-year-old daughter took sick, asked Jesus to come to his house and see about his little girl who was at the point of death. As Jesus was on His way there, He was interrupted by the woman who had an issue of blood for twelve long years. Jesus eventually arrived and healed his child by waking her out of sleep.

In another account, a frantic father met Jesus in Capernaum and told Him about his ailing son. Without being at the son's bedside, Jesus reassured the father that his son would live, and he believed that report the same hour. As the father headed back home, he was told by his servants the good news that his son was indeed alive. Ironically, he asked when they saw signs of improvement; they said, *"Yesterday!"* which was the exact moment He spoke that word.

Lastly, a faithless father brought his disabled son to Jesus' disciples for healing. Unfortunately, those disciples were unsuccessful in helping the deaf and dumb boy with this impending illness because they were incapable without the process of prayer and fasting. Jesus challenged this father to believe again because He knew that all of his efforts at this point were futile, which caused the residue of unbelief to set in. *"Prayer is the key to the kingdom, and faith unlocks the door!"*

We cannot see into the future. We cannot see through dark clouds. We cannot see through teardrops but walk on by faith each day. Take a step on Monday, walk on. Take another step on Tuesday, walk on. Let Jesus be your guide. *He's able to carry your load, He can see way down the road.* Walk on by faith each day. *"For we walk by faith, and not by sight."* I encourage you to believe. All things are possible if you only believe.

I've discussed the accounts of fathers who have their share of withdrawals when dealing with the distress, the disturbances, and the disappointments of our children. These accounts dispel the notion that all men are dogs, unconcerned fathers, and deadbeat dads. The concern, the compassion, and the commitment of these men only prove that after all this time, deposits are still being made.

While some fathers lick the wounds of their inner withdrawals, some fathers find themselves seeking answers from an outer source. This time, I'm not referring to the financial aspects placed on fathers, but I love the way these dutiful dads deposited their children's ailments in the hands of another man. John writes in chapter 1, when acknowledging Jesus as a man, *"whose shoe's latchet I am not worthy to unloose."*

With every withdrawal life takes out of you, a deposit in the proper institution produces and provides interest. There is a better way to handle whatever is on your plate. *"Cast all your cares on the Lord, for He careth for you."* Turn it over to the Lord, and He'll work it out. When it comes to your account, Jesus makes the transfer. Water into wine. Every transaction leads to transitions. Jesus knows how to subtract. He'll take the pain away. Jesus knows how to divide. He helped Moses part the Red Sea. Jesus knows how to multiply. He fed 5,000 with 2 fish and 5 loaves of bread. Jesus knows how to add.

After Job lost everything, He gave him 14,000 sheep, 6,000 oxen, 1,000 cattle, seven sons, and three daughters. Every sacrifice Job made for his children caused God to bless Job in his latter days. No penalties, just profit. No division, just dividends. Not checking, but savings. I've heard the joyful sound: Jesus saves, Jesus saves. To the utmost, Jesus saves. He will pick you up and turn you around. Hallelujah, Jesus saves.

A Rest Stop For The Restless

Matthew 11:28
Come unto me, all ye that labour and are heavy laden, and I will give you rest.

One of the recurring phrases I hear from individuals of different age groups in this culture is, "I'm tired!" Depending on the person, my usual response is, "Tired from what?" When I was younger, I thought I knew what being tired meant. Staying up all night watching television after your parents told you to go to bed. Anybody remember when you were given a bedtime? Playing video games, talking on the phone, or hanging out in the streets knowing you had to get up in a few hours would be reasons one would be tired.

Now that I'm older and have experienced some things, I realize I had no clue of what the true definition of tired meant back then. But now I know I can identify when folk say, "I'm tired!" People all over the world are tired for one reason or another. Tired of working and not seeing the labor reflected in their pockets. Tired of struggling with bills in an economy where making a living gets harder as the days go by. Tired of inconsistency. Tired of two-faced people. Tired of being lied to by politicians in order to get votes, and tired of people in their families who just want your help. Tired of racism. Tired of the instability of our government. Tired of not being able to trust others because their agenda only serves them. Tired of countless black men dying at the hands of law enforcement. Tired of seeing young people with potential, great talent with the ability to achieve goals, throwing their lives away drinking, smoking, chilling on the couch, and hanging out on the corner. Tired of innocent children being abused and treated unfairly. With all this science and technology, there's still no cure for cancer. Old folks used to say, "Just sick and tired of being sick and tired!"

Dealing with these daily dilemmas will leave you tossing and turning all night long, so when that alarm clock goes off, all you can say is, "I'm so tired!" When a person is tired, they're irritable, agitated, frustrated, and easily aggravated. Most people cope with tiredness just by making a run to Dunkin' or Starbucks for a caffeine boost, drinking a can of Red Bull or a bottle of Five Hour Energy to perk up and press on. After a while, they soon find out that artificial fuel is only temporary because nothing lasts forever.

It's difficult to get sleep when there are numerous thoughts on your mind and questions like how, why, who, what, and where are unanswered. What do you do when the stress is so alarming, and the snooze button isn't an option? You find yourself up all night, eating, texting, and panicking. Ask your neighbor, "What's keeping you up?" May I share that your living situation can contribute to your lack of sleep? Children always need something, constantly calling you. Phones won't stop ringing. The demand can literally leave you sleep-deprived. Physicians have diagnosed individuals who can't sleep with insomnia. Insomnia, beloved, is defined as a common sleep disorder characterized by persistent difficulty falling asleep, staying asleep, or experiencing non-restorative sleep. Despite having adequate opportunity for sleep, you still find yourself awake all night long.

It can be considered a disorder when these sleep difficulties cause significant distress or impairment in daily functioning. When the body doesn't get enough sleep, it can malfunction at the wrong times. You can find yourself falling asleep at your desk, on the bus, subway, or even behind the wheel. The lack of sleep is not just a liability to you, but perhaps to someone else as well.

Growing up, I wasn't a morning person. When my mother came into the room, letting me know it was time for school, she turned on all the lights, pulled up the shades, and continued to call my name until I got up. I recall a principle that will help you. I told her, "Ma, I'm up." She said, "You might be up, but you're not out!"

You may be aware of your surroundings, eyes wide open, knowing a change is calling, but still have the difficulty of getting out of what you're in. Psalms 40:2 shares, *"He brought me up also out of an horrible pit, out of the miry clay, And set my feet upon a rock, and established my goings."* God doesn't want you to be just up; He wants you out! *"Being up is good, but being out is better!"*

I heard the saying, "I got up on the wrong side of the bed!" At my very grown age, I still don't know what side is the wrong side. Is it by the window? Is it by the radiator? If your feet hit the floor, you're not on the wrong side; you're on the right. *"Who side are you leaning on?"* Don't know about you, but today I'm not ashamed to admit, "I'm leaning on the Lord's side!" I hear the hymnologist in my ear, *"I'm learning to lean, I'm learning to lean. Finding more power than I've ever needed. I'm learning to lean and depend on Jesus."*

I'm sure you know ten people this morning who know somebody who can stay in bed all day and don't feel bad. Hopefully, you're not that person. Not worried about time or day. Just comfortable with no care in the world. Nothing worse than having to get up early and go to work, leaving someone in bed only to return hours later and they're still in bed. They haven't washed, haven't brushed their teeth, haven't cooked, didn't answer the phone because it's on DND, didn't check the mail. Just sleeping all day. If they're not bedridden, disabled, or homebound, then they're lazy, shiftless, trifling, and reckless. Then they wonder why their life is at a standstill. Staying in bed too long will sap your strength.

You remember in John 5, the lame man had become so attached to the bed that it crippled him from receiving his healing. He lay there for 38 years. After hearing his plethora of excuses, Jesus told the man, *"Rise, pick up your bed, and walk!"* Despite my health challenges, something on the inside won't let me stay in bed past a certain hour. I feel like a failure. A nugget of wisdom shared with me by my pastor that I'll never forget is, *"You can't be great in the bed!"* In other words, nothing will get accomplished if sleeping is the only thing you've mastered. Ephesians 5:14 tells us, *"Wherefore he saith, Awake thou that sleepest, and arise from the dead, and Christ shall give thee light."* Paul writes this verse to the church at Ephesus as a call to Christians to awaken from spiritual slumber and embrace the light of Christ. It encourages believers to recognize the spiritual darkness around them and actively choose to live in the light of God's truth.

Jesus warns us in Matthew 13:25, *"But while men slept, his enemy came and sowed tares among the wheat, and went his way."* Satan lies in wait when you're vulnerable and weak in a semi-conscious state to sow seeds of discord. One can be so unaware that you don't even notice that you're sleeping with the enemy. Have you ever woken up to a nightmare? In the wrong bed? Lying next to a stranger? Jacob will tell you, this ain't Rachel; it's Leah.

I've discovered you can go to sleep and not rest comfortably.

I sense in my spirit that many of you are unsatisfied with the past, unsettled about the present, and unsure about the future. This uneasiness has led you to find other methods and vices because you're restless. Temporary fixes don't solve the problem. You can't drink it away, smoke it away, sex it away, text it away, vacation it away, move away; it's not going away!

The truth is, some of you are scared of the unknown, so your security is in the familiar. You don't want to be disappointed again, so you don't have any expectations. You desire progress, but you worry about the process. Not only are you overwhelmed, but the devil has convinced you that you're all alone. So now you're going through cycles of chaos, patterns of procrastination, and mazes of misery. You're unbothered, with a sign on your heart that reads, *"No Vacancy!"* You're so over it, you won't make a commitment. You can't keep your word. No communication. You are aimlessly walking around like a zombie, lost in the wilderness, going through the motions, defensive, ready to strike, seeking validation, searching for a refuge, looking over your shoulder, questioning every agenda, second-guessing every motive.

This is right where Satan wants you, to pump your brakes and park your car. Even when you've been invited by the girls, the guys, the sorority, or boo, although you go, it's no longer fun. All you can think about is getting back in bed. I know you've been trying to protect your peace; that's just a smoke screen for distance, because peace doesn't need to be protected. Peace is one of the fruits of the Spirit, designed to comfort you.

The comforting words of Jesus in John 14:27 reassure us: *"Peace I leave with you, my peace I give unto you: not as the world giveth, give I unto you. Let not your heart be troubled, neither let it be afraid."* Be mindful of using this feeling as a cloak of maliciousness as well. What is a "cloak of maliciousness?" This phrase, used by the Apostle Peter, means using your exhaustion as an excuse for sinful behavior.

It's a fact: *"Hurt people, hurt people!"* I've learned empty folk will fill up with the wrong stuff. Sin has consequences that will lead you down a path that only a small percentage have come back from. Paul said, *"There's a war in my members."* It's in your members, it's in your memory, and it's in your mannerisms. I know life is lifing, but your stinking thinking got you sinking. Stop fighting spiritual wars with fleshy solutions. Abraham and Sarah are prime examples that don't work. You're not battling just worldly influence; you're suffering from a "weary spirit."

A weary spirit is a state of emotional, spiritual exhaustion and discouragement, often arising from life's challenges and struggles. It signifies a deep-seated fatigue that goes beyond physical tiredness, affecting one's motivation, focus, and overall well-being. In a spiritual context, it can indicate a need for rest, renewal, and introspection. The letdowns of life have shattered our faith. Your faith receptacles have been null and void. The wires have become crossed, and your judgment has become cloudy. The engine light of your soul is on, and a soul-searching diagnostic test is overdue.

When a car is inspected, all areas of the vehicle are checked thoroughly. Cars won't pass inspection if there is any sign of damage or mechanical problems. I know a sticker for a car inspection is good for 2–3 years. When is the last time you had a self-inspection? Psalms 139:23 notes, *"Search me, O God, and know my heart: Try me, and know my thoughts:"* In asking God to search us, we are inviting Him also to open our hearts so that we might receive the conviction of His Spirit. When was the last time you felt convicted, or are you convinced yourself that because you're human, it's okay? The things that you deem are okay will ultimately KO you.

Please do me a favor and mark this date on your calendar. Today is the turning point for you. You've been invited by the Savior to a place where you can finally get your peace back. Get it out of your head; today isn't just another service. Your life is about to take a 180. This text I read is an invitation from Jesus to those who are weary and burdened, promising them rest and relief. RSVP is required, and it's time sensitive. If you fit into this category, then Jesus is talking specifically to you. You may be having a hard time accepting or admitting this truth, but all the signs, signals, and symptoms reveal this is your reality. Jesus, beloved, is making an appeal of comfort, relief, and spiritual renewal to those who are weary, burdened, and feeling the weight of life's challenges.

It's not just a physical rest, but a deeper peace that comes from following Jesus. It's a rest that goes beyond physical exhaustion and addresses the deeper needs of the soul. By coming to Him, surrendering to His guidance, and accepting His teachings, individuals can find rest for their souls. This invitation is not limited to a specific group of people or a particular circumstance; it's an open invitation to all who seek relief from the burdens of life. I've been there. Despite how disciplined you try to be about your bedtime, you can sleep without getting rest.

If you have ever traveled for any length of time, you will eventually need a rest stop. A rest stop is a place where people can stop their vehicles, typically on a highway or long road, to rest, use restrooms, get refreshments, and stretch their legs. It's a designated area designed to provide a safe and convenient place for travelers to take a break and reduce fatigue during their journey.

I know you're in a hot spot. I know the humidity is high, but I came to speak a word to you, the restless, not just to the young and the restless, but if you are one who can't rest. There is a rest stop up ahead, and after today, you'll have proper rest. You've tried to do it and have been unsuccessful. Your greatest efforts have fallen into the ground. God is about to do something that's going to build you up for the road ahead. I know you read signs that say, "Detour and Dead End," but look for the sign, "I'll Give

You Rest." That's where you pull over because God is moving you to the promised place of rejuvenation and restoration. In Psalms 23, David shares, *"He maketh me to lie down in green pastures: He leadeth me beside the still waters. He restoreth my soul."* Secondly, you're being repaired so you can love again. You're being repaired so you can feel alive again. Repaired so you can pass inspection. Lastly, there's recovery. God brought you out of the operating room to the recovery room. Rest. Repairs. Recovery. All of this will take place at the rest stop. So, if you're restless, put your signal on; this is your exit.

Closed Doors Don't Matter

Mark 2:1-5

And again he entered into Capernaum after some days; and it was noised that he was in the house. And straightway many were gathered together, insomuch that there was no room to receive them, no, not so much as about the door: and he preached the word unto them. And they come unto him, bringing one sick of the palsy, which was borne of four. And when they could not come nigh unto him for the press, they uncovered the roof where he was: and when they had broken it up, they let down the bed wherein the sick of the palsy lay. When Jesus saw their faith, he said unto the sick of the palsy, Son, thy sins be forgiven thee.

Unfortunately, everywhere you look, things are closing down all around us. Businesses are closing. Houses are foreclosing. There are lane and street closures because of flooding. Every time we close our eyes and wake the next morning, another executive order has been signed by this current administration at 1600 Pennsylvania Ave. Banks and hospitals are closed because of the massive increase in layoffs. Federal programs and universities are closing due to lack of funding. Sadly, years after the pandemic, some houses of worship are still closed. We're in need of some help, and there is nothing worse than needing help only to find folk standing on the outside looking in. Can't get help from helping hands. Can't afford the bus fare to get to the welfare. SNAP has been snatched. Child care is unaffordable. Everywhere you go, there's a closed door being slammed in your face. Medicaid and Medicare are being eliminated. The Department of Education is under attack, and the bills are piling high. When people see your plight and offer you help, we've allowed pride to set in. I've discovered that closed mouths don't get fed.

You may be wondering where you fit in with things closing daily. There is an unsettling feeling when trying to find your place. I hear the songwriter making an inquiry: Where do I go when there's no one else to turn to? Who do I talk to when there's no one else to listen? Who do I lean on when there's no stable foundation? I go to the rock. I know He's able. I go to the rock. I go to the rock of my salvation. I go to the stone that the builders rejected. I run to the mountain, and the mountain stands by me. When all around me is sinking sand, on Christ the solid rock I stand. When I need a shelter, when I need a friend, I go to the rock. Shake a neighbor's hand and tell them, "I Go To The Rock!" Can you say, "Glory To God!"

We're indeed living in the last days, and those are upon us even now. Every time you turn on the radio, the television, or open up the newspaper, you hear of death, destruction, and devastation. Folks have isolated themselves. They're still in their own personal quarantine. The doors are locked because of ICE agents, and calls are blocked because of scams. People are living in fear because of the threat of another virus strain. Individuals are just trying to survive, make it from one day to another, and the plan of the enemy is to make our lives a living hell. While Satan is plotting, God still has a master plan. I've got some good news for you.

In the last days, there's a promise that God will pour out His

Spirit on all flesh. The economy may be declining, but the Spirit of God is on the rise. Listen, nobody told me the road would be easy. Do you still believe God hasn't brought you this far to leave you now? There must be a solution for this revolution. If ever we needed the Lord before, we sure do need Him now. Do you need the Lord? Do your children need Him? Take a moment and say to yourself, "I Need The Lord!"

There's a dire need in our text above. Mark, the disciple, paints a vivid portrait of a crowd that desperately needed a touch from Jesus. In those days, there wasn't access to social media messaging, a group text, or an email blast yet, and people used word of mouth, causing hundreds, perhaps thousands, to gather all because they heard that Jesus was in Capernaum again. This wasn't His first visit to the City of Comfort. During His time there, He preached after being tempted in the wilderness by the Devil. It was in Capernaum that He called Levi from his tax collector's booth. In this city, the Centurion's servant was healed after the urgent request of his master. He also healed Peter's mother-in-law from her sickbed. With that type of résumé, no wonder folk were looking to be added to the list of miracles.

Jesus' fame spread abroad, and so many people came to the house that it was standing room only. It was packed from the pulpit to the door. Wouldn't it be wonderful if folk would fill up the churches again? Not for anniversaries, not for clubs or rallies, not for business meetings, but because Jesus is in the building. Some people come to church for the wrong reasons and focus on the wrong things. A story is told of a woman who was new to the church, and after three months, she told the Pastor one Sunday after service, it was her last Sunday there.

The pastor, concerned about her decision, inquired what was going on. She told him that when she came to church, she couldn't help but notice individuals texting instead of praying. When she went to the restroom, she heard saints gossiping about others, and people were laughing while others were praising. All this was a real turn-off for her. The pastor said he understood her reasons, but asked her to do him a favor before she left. He told her to come next week with a glass full of water. The request seemed strange, but the following week, she came through the door with a glass full of water. The pastor asked her during the service to walk around the sanctuary without spilling the water. When service was over, he asked if she enjoyed her worship experience. She responded, "Well, I heard the choir sing and heard you preach."

The pastor wondered if she noticed the laughing, the texting, and the gossiping. She said, "No, I was too busy being sure I didn't spill the water in the glass." When your focus is on your assignment, then you don't have time to look at what others are doing. Jesus, you're the center of my joy; all that's good and perfect comes from You. When Jesus is your main focus, let folk talk, let individuals laugh, and let people text, but a charge to keep I have and a God to glorify. If my mother don't go and my father don't go, if my siblings don't go, I'll go anyway.

As Jesus was ministering, a man with a condition called palsy was being carried by four of his friends. In the Bible, "palsy" is a condition of paralysis that is a debilitating weakness of the muscles, often resulting in the inability to move or function normally. There are people who may not be officially diagnosed with palsy, but when they come to church, they don't move. They won't shake a neighbor's hand. Some won't even speak. They never lift their hands, never open their mouths, never praise God. They just sit on the premises when they should be standing on the promises. When was the last time you praised God? There are Christians who believe it doesn't take all that. Let them watch the Knicks, Jets, or Giants, and you'll see the statues in church come alive. I'm a sports fan too, but when I think of the goodness of Jesus and all He's done for me, my soul cries out, "Hallelujah!" Praise God, praise God. Praise Him in the morning, praise Him in the noon-

ICU

day. Praise God, praise God. Praise Him when the sun goes down.

Let me close this chapter with this. These four friends were determined to get their friend the help he needed. The door was closed. The place was packed. Under normal circumstances, people would have left. Others would have been discouraged by the number of people, but these four friends wouldn't be denied. Could you imagine what kind of church this would be if someone came not just for a blessing but to help someone else get theirs? I know things are closing down. Morale is down. Support is down. But shake yourself and speak over your own life as you're reading this and declare, "Things May Be Shut Down, But We're Not Shut Out!" I'm writing this to encourage you and to let you know that there's another way.

Closed doors don't matter. The door may be locked. The door may be blocked. Remember, after the resurrection of Jesus, Thomas didn't believe that Jesus had returned from the dead. The room the disciples were in was closed, and Jesus walked through the door and showed Thomas His scars and wounds from the cross. I need to get to Jesus no matter what. They decided to tear off the roof and help their friend get his breakthrough.

Whatever is standing in the way of my answer has got to be broken up. Cliques gotta be broken up. Posses gotta be broken up. Entitlement gotta be broken up. I gotta get to Jesus. Ain't no mountain high enough, ain't no valley low enough, ain't no river wide enough to keep me from getting to You. You can get there by railway. You can get there by trailway. I don't care how you get there, just get there if you can. All day long, Satan has been trying to keep you from getting here. Children acting up. Bus running late. Nothing to wear. Access-A-Ride stuck in traffic. All this was designed to make you change your mind about what God said He will do in your life. The Devil is aware that this is your season; that's why he's been fighting you so hard.

Let me remind you that "God Has A Blessing For You!" You can have it, reach up and grab it. When you think of all the hell you've been through in the past year—through the obstacles, through the hurdles, through the aches and through the pain, through the tears—scream, "Somehow, I Made It!" I had to be here because "Closed Doors Don't Matter!" Jesus saw the faith. Jesus marveled at their perseverance. Jesus witnessed their persistence and healed the man. If you press your way, God will heal you.

Is there anything too hard for God? Have you any mountains that you can't tunnel through? Are there any rivers that seem uncrossable? God specializes in things that seem impossible, and He will do what no other power can do. Peter didn't let a closed door stop him when he was in prison. I went to the hospital the other day to visit one of the mothers in Zion. As I approached the door, I noticed there was no button, no handle, no push bar. But to my amazement, the door opened on its own. The Holy Ghost told me to tell you that you won't have to pull or push, break it down, or pick the lock. All you need to do for the rest of the year is put your foot in the right spot, and doors will open automatically. Every place the sole of your foot shall tread upon, I'll give you that place.

Stay in position. Be in the right place. Stay on your post and watch God open doors that you never thought you would walk into. Social Security may have denied you. The bank may have denied you. The bursar's office may have denied your application. The dealership may have denied you. So watch where you place your foot and get ready to walk into your new season, because closed doors don't matter.

www.ingramcontent.com/pod-product-compliance
Lightning Source LLC
Chambersburg PA
CBHW050704160426
43194CB00010B/1989